Launch to Impact

Essential Foundations to Optimize Your Influence and Accelerate Success as a Developing Leader

Keena R. Mosley, EdD

ISBN: 979-8-9872482-2-5
E-ISBN: 979-8-9872482-3-2

In order to maintain confidentiality, certain names, locations, and identifying characteristics have been changed or omitted. These modifications are made to protect the privacy of individuals and institutions. Any similarity to real persons or entities is purely coincidental unless explicitly noted.

Because of the dynamic nature of the internet, any web addresses or links contained in this book may have changed since publication and may no longer be valid.The views expressed in this work are solely those of the author.

Printed in the United States of America

To access the *Launch Point Journal*, which includes a
wealth of information and resources to help
you on your leadership journey, please
visit www.launchtoimpact.org.

Table Of Contents

Introduction

Welcome to *Launch to Impact*! If you are reading this book, you are likely an aspiring or newly promoted leader. I am hopeful that the content contained throughout these pages will provide you with opportunities to carefully consider some core foundational issues as you develop and move forward on your leadership journey so that you can confidently face the challenges that lie ahead, providing critical guidance to team members.

Right now, you may lack the confidence and support—or the right people—to ask questions about leadership, what it entails, what the process looks like, and how you can move forward without feeling intimidated by those conversations. Oftentimes, team members may appear to lack initiative or are unsure of themselves, but it's simply because they don't have opportunities to ask the questions they need answered or it is because they lack confidence. Many times, those who I encounter don't want to interrupt, inconvenience, or burden their busy leader, so they don't always know who to approach for support.

Be sure to avoid making comparisons to more seasoned leaders. Every leader started exactly where you are, and every leader—no matter their level—needs support, encouragement, and a network. This book will provide you with all of those things and give you the voice you may feel like you don't have to speak up for yourself.

I have served in many different leadership roles and have been instrumental in developing a number of leaders over the years. With more than twenty years of experience in leadership, much of my time has been spent cultivating new and aspiring leaders. I have a doctoral degree in organizational and educational leadership, and my master's degree in organizational leadership. Most recently, I founded a consulting firm where I specifically focus on developing and coaching leaders at all levels. As I reflect on my professional journey, I realize that I was fortunate enough to have strong leaders that poured into me throughout my entire career. Many people don't have that.

My experience includes serving as the Deputy Director for a program serving over 2,000 children with an annual budget of $20 million. I have held leadership positions at the county level where I provided multidisciplinary guidance to as many as thirteen different programs simultaneously. Additionally, I have helped early education leaders get their federally-funded programs out of deficient compliance status and make the necessary changes to operate efficiently and effectively. Moreover, I have turned organizations around and improved their organizational culture. Because of all of these feats, I have the qualifications necessary to support new leaders.

Since I've always had supportive leadership, I felt alone and abandoned the one time I didn't. During that time, I second-guessed everything I did. I doubted myself in ways that I had never doubted myself before. But the moment that I was able to get support, all of the doubts disappeared. Not only did I feel empowered and encouraged, but I also experienced greater success.

As you read this book, I want you to feel like you have the support you need to soar and become the leader you envision. I want you to get to the point where you have team members that truly believe in you so that they push you forward while you push them. This way, everybody goes up together.

When I was working with someone who was not a strong or supportive leader in their organization, it was very difficult for me to teach them the skills they needed to get everyone in alignment with their vision and direction. I'm saying this to say that I've never been unsuccessful at making an impact on the people that I was tasked to lead, but I have been in a situation where I didn't have an impact on my leader and direct supervisor. I've almost always been in positions where my leader came to me for advice; I've always had an impact on my leader, whether directly or indirectly. Leaders who have reported to me saw results in their ability to push through challenging situations, maintain their integrity, exercise discipline, and remain focused in the midst of adversity. Ultimately, they saw that progress wasn't a straight line.

As a leader, you have to show up. You consistently have to do your job and model all of the things that you expect from your team members. I worked with a program that spent half a million dollars on substitutes one year. They spent so much money on substitutes because morale was down and the staff didn't want to go to work. Nobody wanted to be there, so after changing the organizational structure and culture, I completely eliminated that expense. Employees became happy, so they came to work and did their jobs well.

I also worked with a major university to strengthen their organizational structure and leadership team. I coached them through the federal review process, which they completed successfully. Because of the work the team and I were able to tackle, the university had no deficiencies. To be fair, they had much of what they needed in some form or another, but they lacked the cohesion and direction to bring it together. Some leaders even lacked the confidence to be able to clearly articulate their work to a federal reviewer. This is why *Launch to Impact* is so important.

The purpose of this book is to help new, aspiring, and newly promoted leaders really see their impact, supporting them as they work to elevate their careers and optimize their influence. The advice I share works because it's practical and can be implemented immediately. You don't even have to finish the chapter before you begin to apply what you are reading and achieve tangible results.

I've been where you are. I've worked my way up the proverbial ladder. Nobody gave me anything. I've had to work hard to earn everything that I have accomplished, so I understand how you feel. If you procrastinate on implementing what you learn throughout this book, you won't be able to recognize the results you need. Reading *Launch to Impact* is going to help accelerate your impact and success. However, not reading this book or failing to put the strategies and foundations into practice is going to slow your progress. You will also miss out on opportunities, continue to lack confidence, and continue to be frustrated in your career.

After reading this book and putting these strategies into practice, you are going to have a renewed sense of confidence, understand who you are in ways that you never have before, and be able to navigate the workplace with much more ease and assurance. You won't use the techniques one time; these are strategies that will last your entire leadership journey. Embrace them. Hold them close to you. Leave a positive personal and professional impact on all who come in contact with you. This is your time to *LAUNCH TO IMPACT!*

— Dr. Keena

More Than A Title

"If your actions inspire others to dream more, learn more, do more and become more, you are a leader."
— *John Quincy Adams*

Spoiler alert: The check and title are never enough.

Whether you are at the beginning of your journey or somewhere along the way, you may think about a specific role, contemplate your personal ambitions, or aspire to receive a certain pay rate when considering leadership. You may also consider many other things. At its core, leadership is so much more than what you do for yourself or the goals you want to achieve. Leadership is not just about a title, position, office, or box on an organizational chart. At its essence, leadership is about influence.

In my career, I have had the opportunity to continuously move up the career ladder. This success has been due to both my work ethic and my ability to cultivate relationships. Being fully transparent, I didn't see my-self as a leader when my career began. When I only had a bachelor's degree, people encouraged me to further my education so I could go higher in leadership. Despite the absence of an advanced degree, opportunities were often presented, and I was effective in a number of capacities.

As I consider my early years, I now realize that my influence outweighed my positions. But it wasn't until the position and influence aligned that I was able to reach my full potential. For me, this also meant being elevated to a new position every 2-6 years- with one promotion occurring in approximately 90 days. The difference between my journey and that of others is that I was given opportunities to prepare for the next position before I had secured it. I also realize that the workforce often does not effectively prepare for leadership shifts, which makes transitions much more fragmented than necessary.

In 2023, Forbes reported a 55% increase in CEOs leaving their positions (Hayes, 2024). There are many reasons why this may still be the case today, but ultimately, this statistic is a reminder that titles are temporary. As you chart your unique leadership path, it is important to be mindful that you are on an ever-evolving journey. Leadership is not a destination. Leadership is about who you are and the impact you have on people, systems, strategies, and organizations. When you view your leadership journey as a lifelong commitment to growth, you will remain impactful. If you are in a place where top leaders are leaving their positions at high rates, it creates a domino effect for promotions and organizational restructuring. Be prepared when the dominos inevitably fall in your direction.

When you're thinking about your next career steps, do not consider what seat you will sit in, how far you will ascend on the organizational chart, or even the title you will have. Focus instead on the measure of influence and impact you will have. Leadership is about the mark you will leave on this world, moving things and/or people from one place to another. When they understand their power, good—even great—leaders leave things better than they found them.

There are several different types of power. I want to focus on two: influential power and positional power. Influential power works beyond a position. It belongs to the person who does not have the big cubicle, office, or title, yet people defer to him or her. This is the person that people lean on or look to for guidance. In contrast, positional power refers to the person who has the office, title, and bigger cubicle—all the things that are associated with being in charge. But just because you have the position does not mean you always have the power.

You can see the dynamic between these two powers in many aspects of life. In families, there's always one sibling who seems to lead the entire clan. On the school playground, there's always one child everyone rallies around and follows, even if what they're doing isn't right. At work, there's always one team member who, regardless of what the boss says or what others think, people will watch for his or her reaction or ask for his or her opinion. Others will even wait to see how these leaders respond before deciding whether to participate in some initiatives.

Influence without position is still power. A position without influence, however, is just a box on an organizational chart, so it can be extremely difficult to hold a position without influence. You can get people to do things when you have positional power without influence, but most times, they do it out of obligation, not because they're truly engaged or invested. This type of commitment does not yield the results you truly desire. The best leaders capitalize on their influence to gain a position.

When I think of influence and power, two people come to mind: Dr. Martin Luther King, Jr. and Steve Jobs. Dr. King was, without contest, the most powerful person in the Civil Rights Movement; however, not enough attention is given to how he started making an impact. In 1954, he began pastoring in Montgomery, Alabama. The following year, he led the 381-day Montgomery Bus Boycott. But it wasn't until 1963 that he delivered his famous "I Have a Dream" speech at the Lincoln Memorial in Washington, D.C. As a local pastor, Dr. King's position was specific to his congregation. However, it was his influence in the community that opened the doors for him to lead the bus boycott and the Southern Christian Leadership Conference. It was (and still is) his influence that has stood the test of time and made him a respected world leader.

Apple co-founder Steve Jobs held a position (without enough influence), and although very much a visionary, his board of directors felt he lacked the interpersonal leadership skills to move the company forward. As a result, Jobs was fired in 1985. In 1997, he returned as CEO with both influence and position. Upon his return, Apple went into what seemed to be hyperdrive. Since then, the legacy of both the company and the once-fired founder has forever been branded amongst the most influential in the world.

Influence without position lacks authority. Position without influence lacks potency. Influence, along with position, produces lasting impact.

> *Influence without position lacks authority. Position without influence lacks potency.*

Like Dr. King and Steve Jobs, you must understand that being a leader with influence requires that you focus on connection over control. Leadership is about more than hitting metrics or achieving personal success; it's about leaving a meaningful impact.

Success Is Not Enough: Leaders Must Have Significance

Depending on how you define success, it may be measured by promotions or accolades, but significance is about how your leadership transforms others and drives long-term progress. Significance occurs when you focus on creating value for others, not just yourself, celebrating their successes to amplify their contributions. When your leadership has significance, it will outlast your tenure and inspire others to carry the vision forward.

What does all of this mean? Quite simply, if you want to go far, you need to work on your influence. Success is not enough if you want to make a difference. You must also have significance. Significance is about your track record, how you make other people feel, and how you show up in the world. If you're going to be successful, you must understand that your significance is more than a list of tasks or achievements.

Are you doing things that matter? Of all that you are tasked with, are you doing the right things? Are you doing things that will last? Are you doing work that makes a difference in the lives of your team members? Are you an agent of change? This is the crux of significance. As you enter this new or next phase of leadership, identify what is most important in your context by paying attention to other leaders.

Study Leaders Around You

Leadership lessons are all around you. By observing the leaders in your network, workplace, or industry, you can gain valuable insights into what works—and what doesn't—along with the "why" behind their efforts. The more you study other leaders and make needed adaptations to fit your current context, the better equipped you will be to navigate your own leadership challenges.

As you engage in this study, adopt a stance of curiosity in which you seek knowledge with a growth mindset. This will help you ask the right questions and gain an understanding of the nuances that inform and shape decisions. Be attentive to both what happens on the surface and what goes on behind the scenes. This will help you determine how you'll show up as a leader, which practices you'll adopt, and the strategies you'll set aside. Maybe, over time, you'll revisit some of them and decide to use them when the time is right, or maybe you won't because they no longer suit you, your team, or the times you are functioning in.

As a child, you probably aspired to be like your parents, your teachers, or other people who influenced you and left their mark on your soul. However, as a leader, you need to figure out who you want to emulate. Who will you follow? Who will you listen to? Who will lead you? These decisions will play a significant role in shaping the kind of leader you ultimately become.

Any successful leader will tell you that no single approach works well for every situation or team member. In fact, possessing a variety of skills and the ability to draw

> *No single approach works well for every situation*

on different values and characteristics to meet each moment is of the utmost importance.

In my first—and only—internship, I was fortunate enough to spend a little more than a year with a young educator who, for all intents and purposes, was everything I thought I wanted to be. She looked like me, sounded like me, and was incredibly successful. Admired by many, she was a successful educator at her university and recognized as someone worthy of pouring into the lives of new educators to help them forge their paths. So, I began to pattern myself after my mentor-teacher. That is, until everything seemed to turn in a different direction. And when I say "everything," I mean *everything*.

My mentor-teacher and I spent lots of time together, both at school and after school, where she shared resources and experiences with me, even showing me aspects of life beyond work. These moments allowed me to start shaping a vision for what I wanted my own future to look like. I admired and revered her to some degree until the day my university professor visited the classroom. My mentor-teacher began talking about how much she had done to assist me to the point where it seemed like I contributed absolutely nothing. She really began to chip away at and tear down what I had begun to build as a new educator. As a result, I was called to campus about my alleged lack of performance and I completely lost trust in her.

Choosing to no longer rely on my mentor-teacher, I began pulling together my own resources. If you know anything about being an intern—especially in education—you know access to resources is limited. For my classroom, I needed a lot of materials. I was so determined that I didn't even ask my mentor-teacher for a box of crayons. Instead, I relied on my classmates and family members for supplies.

With the exception of the debt that I accumulated, this period of time worked out in my favor in the long run. As I went further into my career, I realized I needed more stamina. I needed access to resources and became creative by repurposing materials. I also realized that if given the responsibility for developing other educators, I would never put them in the position I had been placed in.

Oftentimes, positive examples of leaders are the only ones that come to mind. These are the people everyone wants to be like, but please do not discount the immense value of the non-example. Non-examples can save you from experiencing considerable pain and suffering, ensuring that you remain true to your values, beliefs, and nature. Pay attention to the non-examples because they have the ability to take you just as far as those you want to pattern yourself after.

Have an Accurate View of Self

At the heart of effective leadership is self-awareness. Leaders who understand their strengths, limitations, and impact on others are better positioned to grow and lead authentically. An accurate view of self is not about perfection; it's about humili-

> *As a leader, it is essential to have an accurate view of yourself.*

ty and the willingness to evolve. So, I recommend that you do three things as you continue to grow and serve as a leader: go to therapy, keep a journal, and regularly spend time in deep reflection. As a leader, it is essential to have an accurate view of yourself. A leader who lacks self-awareness can be detrimental to themselves and others.

I think of a new leader I had the opportunity to mentor. Hillary, a supervisor in an entry-level role, had been in that position for quite some time. Once I became the person she reported to, I got to know her and her teammates. After noticing certain skills and character traits in her, I realized Hillary was serving beneath her purpose; she wasn't working to her full capacity. Quite honestly, I also began to realize that the organization we both worked for at the time was too small for her. Hillary needed to spread her wings, gain more influence, and get experience in a different setting to truly discover who she was and how far she could go.

From my perspective, Hillary had kind of settled for where she was as if it were the end of her career journey, but I saw something more in her. So, I took an unconventional approach—something I often do—and encouraged her to apply for a job outside of the organization.

The job I suggested wasn't necessarily a promotional opportunity; it was a similar role to the one she held at the time. However, the position had a larger scope.

When I made my recommendation, Hillary was nervous, but I told her that I had full confidence in her and would write her a strong recommendation letter. Above all, I needed her to trust me. And she did. Hillary took the leap, applied for a job at an organization where I had previously worked, got hired, and performed exceptionally well. Before long, Hillary moved on to receive a promotion in a different organization. She went from entry-level supervisor to principal.

Since the time of her employment change, Hillary has been identified as a leader that can successfully turn a school around. But for her to reach the point of understanding that even being a principal is not her final destination, Hillary had to get a better view of herself. She needed to stop defining herself based on the environment she was in at the time. She had to gain a more accurate viewpoint of her skills and recognize what she brought to the table. She did the work. She did the reflection, the journaling, and everything else necessary to prove to herself that she could do it. Because of this, Hillary's career soared. She no longer feels frustrated or stagnant. She even had the opportunity to transfer from one school to another because she had accomplished all that was needed at her first stop. Therefore, the administration needed Hillary to take her magic to the next school site.

I have also had multiple experiences with several leaders who lacked self-awareness; fortunately for you, I will only share one - it is the one that I wanted to turn around the most and still have lasting regrets about. Greg was a leader who continuously wanted to separate himself from others in the leadership team by expressing the level of authority his position had and also requested that his superiors communicate the authority that his position held. He spoke to others in a dismissive tone and would refuse to work with certain people. When given opportunities to expand his responsibility, he would refuse to learn from the people that were assigned to support him because he wanted this "training" to come from someone more respected in his eyes. His leader, along with multiple consultants (me included) attempted to make headway, but to no avail. Greg was great at pointing the finger at others, but unwilling to do anything about how he was showing up and damaging the morale of the organization. Once Greg was no longer in the organization, morale instantly increased, and working dynamics improved. As for my regrets, the truth is - you can't help someone that doesn't wnat to be helped and refuses to do the work. This lack of self-awareness is the type of thing that can handicap your career and cause you to leave destruction everywhere you go.

Here are a few things you can do to get an accurate view of yourself and define who you want to be as a leader:

First, reflect on the leaders you've had in your past to figure out the things about them that you want to adopt for yourself or be cautious of.

Next, review your successes. Identify the places where you have truly made an impact on others and how you did it. This will help you recognize what you've genuinely accomplished. It's easy to become so busy and bogged down in work without stopping to realize the true scope of your impact.

Then, look at your reference letters. I highly recommend keeping all your reference letters, cards, acknowledgments, and notes of appreciation.

No matter how old or distant they might be, hold on to anything containing kind things people have said about you when they didn't have to. In your moments of frustration—when you're trying to figure out who you are, what you should be doing, and how you show up in the world—those letters and acknowledgments will help you see how others perceive you. Serving as both confirmation and redirection, those written recommendations will help you realize the impact you've had on others' lives. I even recommend that my clients create an acknowledgement folder in their email inbox. This is where they save any emails they receive about their success and impact. These are messages that they will receive from people who will not likely be the author of a reference letter and will help them to see how they are viewed by colleagues and subordinates.

After that, take a personal inventory to identify the types of things people repeatedly ask you for. People rely on you for different things but every person has a core skill that everyone connected to them takes note of. As a leader, your leadership shows up everywhere you go. To conduct your personal inventory, start by asking your colleagues, team members, supervisors, managers, family members, and friends probing questions. You can ask, "What is it that you rely on me for? What do you depend on me to do that you don't typically depend on others for?" Their answers will reveal some of your greatest strengths, along with the unique ways your leadership benefits others. Your respondents will highlight the things you consistently do and the ways you regularly show up. These attributes are often the things that come easiest to you—the things you might consider simple, insignificant or take for granted. Understand that, for those on the receiving end of your greatness, these characteristics are important. To truly recognize your value and influence, you need to have an accurate view of yourself and a vision of who you want to be as a leader.

Define Who You Want to Be as a Leader

Every leader must answer a fundamental question: Who do I want to be in this role? Having this level of clarity and conviction is not about emulating or conforming to the expectations of others; it's about intentionally defining your leadership character, values, and personality.

The less experience you have, the more foreign this foundation will seem. Conversely, the more responsibility you have, the more crucial it is to decide who you want to be as a leader.

Before I figured out that I was called to education, I somehow convinced myself that it was a "poor man's career." Though I liked working with kids and making them smile, I didn't really know if there was a deeper meaning or purpose beyond that. In an effort to prepare for my best life, I originally planned to pursue a career in accounting. That is, until I took a gap year before college to work at a restaurant.

A new Chuck E. Cheese was being built in my city, so I immediately applied for a position before the restaurant even opened. I got hired and was an inaugural team member. As a cashier who also worked other positions, I was heavily relied on in those opening months. I did everything required of my position and, in typical fashion, went above and beyond. I helped the new staff and other team members, supported the managers, and learned about many different areas in the restaurant. I did whatever was needed for myself and the team.

At some point, it became time for the managers to identify and select team leaders. As a team leader, I would receive a blue shirt to wear with my khakis, making me stand out among the rest of the group members who wore red shirts. I was completely confident that I would be amongst the newly minted team leaders because everyone relied on me. My coworkers came to me to solve problems, get assistance, and receive needed support. I already did all of the things a team leader would be tasked to do. Because of this, I knew I had the position in the bag.

One morning, I pulled up to work, and as other team members were getting out of their vehicles, I started to see a series of blue shirts. Disappointed that my shirt was still red, I immediately got that sinking feeling of rejection in my stomach; my entire body instantly became heavy. Despite the weight of emotions that overwhelmed me, I bottled it all up, shifted my focus and went to work.

Sometime in the middle of my shift, one of the assistant managers I had a strong relationship with came to me and said he wanted to speak with me at the end of the day. I just looked at him, acknowledged his request, and figured he wanted to talk to me about the shirts. At that point, though, I felt like him giving me a shirt—if that was his intention—was an afterthought. The feelings of rejection had already settled in.

Nonetheless, I went to talk to this assistant manager at the end of my shift. He began to apologize and explained the deliberation process the managers engaged in when selecting who to promote. Not only did shirts change but raises were given. I listened intently to my assistant manager before finally speaking up. "Can you just tell me why I didn't get it? That's really all I want to know."

My manager said something that triggered a struggle I have had my entire life. He said, "This is supposed to be like Disney. This is supposed to be one of the happiest places in a child's life, and smiles are important. And quite honestly, Keena, you don't smile enough."

I thought, *What? Wait, that's it? I don't smile enough?!*

Not only did I work extra hours and stretch myself, but I also helped the team build the restaurant. I was flexible. I did everything that was asked of me and then some. And the reason I wasn't promoted to team leader was because I didn't smile enough?

He continued, "Sometimes, you have to stretch yourself beyond yourself to get ahead."

I responded, "I'm just not a smiler."

I learned a valuable lesson from that experience. You see, I am not a natural smiler. Some people always look happy. I could be elated but not show it on my facial expression. In fact, the phenomenon best used to describe it is called resting b*tch face (RBF). I'm not trying *not* to smile. It's just my natural facial expression. I have carried what my assistant manager said in my heart, mind, and leadership toolkit since that day.

As the conversation progressed, my assistant manager emphasized that I needed to start smiling if I wanted to get ahead because there was nothing that he could say or do to get the rest of the managers to bet on me. At first, I was absolutely devastated because I felt like there was no way for me to get ahead; I was always going to wear a red shirt simply because I could not smile. But over time, I realized I could smile. In fact, I smile when things make me happy or when I have a reason to smile.

So, I had to dig deep within myself and make some changes. I did some real self-reflection and realized that what I was being asked to do was to change how I showed up, not who I was. I could still be true to who I was yet carry myself a bit differently to move ahead. This small, yet profound, lesson has carried me through my career. Sometimes, it's not the big things you're missing. Sometimes, it's just the small things. But if those small things align with a big value, then it's worth the stretch.

In the end, this assistant manager, along with another manager, began to mentor me. They started helping me with the way I communicated with others. They guided me so that I was ready to be considered the next time a promotion became available. I am proud to say that after a few months under their tutelage, I received my blue shirt.

Even when I left the organization and returned, I quickly received another blue shirt because, despite the smile that may or may not have been on my face, I was an exceptional employee, hard worker, and team player. Though I did not have a sunny disposition, I always did what was necessary for the team to win. And that was something no one could deny me.

During the time when I still wore a red shirt, people came to me for guidance, my opinion, and all the things a leader provided. Ultimately, influence is much more important than a position. Influence isn't bestowed upon you; it is part of the fabric of your very being, your DNA, and the way you operate. When you are navigating your work environment and team relationships, your influence is always going to show up. It's important to understand that influence can take you further than a position ever will.

Many times, people think of a leader as someone who consistently exercises authority by telling people what to do. That's a more top-down approach. However, as you continue to evolve in this world, a top-down approach is not always the best way to lead. You can't lead by saying, "Do as I say, not as I do." Your team members and employees are watching you, and what they want to see from you is what you expect from them. When they see you model what you expect, you'll build your influence and impact. Modeling is how you shape culture, demonstrate what you want your team to focus on, and highlight what is most important. Your words have power and authority, but your actions will take you much further than words ever could.

This is why it's important to decide who you want to be as a leader. If you desire to be a leader who just issues commands, there's a place for that, but it won't build true engagement. If you choose to be a leader who completely relies on your team members and trusts them wholeheartedly without getting your hands dirty, there's a place for that too, but quite honestly, it won't get you far because there are times when even the most skilled team members need their leader to step up. If you want to be a leader who works shoulder-to-shoulder with your team, there's a place for that as well, but understand that without boundaries, always being on your team's level comes at a cost.

The best leaders are able to move in and out of these roles as needed. You have to decide who you want to be and the legacy you want to leave on this Earth. You determine the imprint you want to make in your career and industry. Once you have made this decision, then—and only then—are you truly positioned to develop and adopt a leadership philosophy, knowing who you are and how you will wield both your influence and your position. From there, you can make demands on your team members once they see you living up to the standards that are in place for them.

Model What You Want to See

Leadership is as much about action as it is about vision. Your team looks to you to set the tone; your behavior shapes the culture, values, and expectations of the organization. By modeling the behaviors you want to see, you create a culture of alignment and excellence. Being an effective leader requires continued steps of learning, adapting, and growing. And as you grow in leadership, you will come to understand that these steps toward significance are not a destination; leadership is a journey that includes a series of stops.

> *Leadership is as much about action as it is about vision.*

If you got in your car right now and said, "I am headed to the mountains for a weekend getaway," you might stop at a few places along the way. You might stop for gas, which is important. You might stop to grab a bite to eat, which is necessary. You might even stop to take in some scenery, which is enjoyable. All of these stops are part of the journey. And each place is, in fact, a destination of its own. But your ultimate goal is to reach something greater.

Leadership is a lot like planning a trip. You have an ultimate destination in mind, but along the way, there will be a series of steps or smaller destinations. There will be a series of positions that will help you reach your ultimate goal. And as you continue on your journey, you will encounter decisions, interactions, people and projects that will help you create and build your significance. Likewise, every time you reach a new stage of the journey, you elevate the same mindset and core strategies that you employed in the previous stage. This journey isn't a straight line; it is a cycle that keeps taking you higher.

Leadership Influence (™) Compass

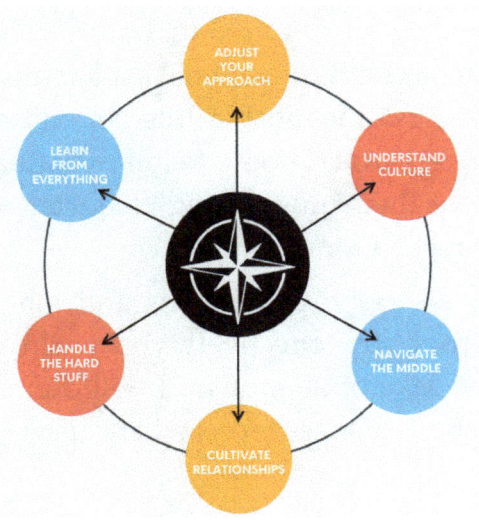

At every stage of your leadership journey, you will need to employ the foundations covered in this book. Your implementation process and the associated strategies you incorporate will evolve as your level of leadership increases, but the following core of the foundation remains consistent:

- Learn from everything
- Adjust your approach
- Understand the power of culture
- Navigate the middle
- Cultivate relationships
- Handle the hard stuff

On the surface, your position is a space on an organizational chart, but to get to what matters most, you need to be clear on what separates positional leadership from influential leadership. A title may grant authority, but influence builds trust and respect. People will follow a title because they are required to, but the depth of their commitment has limits. Positional leadership is effective in some ways, but the most lasting commitment comes from influence. People choose to follow influential leaders because of their unwavering character, impressive results, and regard for others.

In today's society, promotions and long-term success come from how effectively you wield your influence. For the sake of alignment, I will define influence and impact. Both of these terms will be used throughout this book, so there should be a shared understanding of how they will be used.

- Influence - the power or capacity to move others

- Impact - a tangible or intangible result that comes from one's influence

If you reflect on your experiences, I am sure you can find everyday leaders that have been able to influence others in the simplest or most profound ways. You, too, can be this for those within your sphere of influence because you understand and embody that leadership is more than a title, authority, or personal success. A title won't hold your attention, fulfill your soul, or fuel your legacy. It may open doors, but your actions will inspire others. Success fades, but significance leaves a lasting legacy.

Ultimately, the most impactful leaders are those who know themselves, invest in others, and lead with purposeful intentionality.

Note: At the conclusion of each chapter, I provide a few launch points that will guide you in making immediate application of the strategies covered. Review these launch points and be sure to download the bonus resources listed. These materials will help you process, develop, and think through the strategies prior to implementation.

CHAPTER 1 LAUNCH POINTS

Visit www.launchtoimpact.org to access the Influence vs. Position Activity in your Launch Points Journal. To really hone in on or refine your influence, begin with these steps:

1. Identify 2-3 leaders that you admire and determine what qualities you are most drawn to and why.

2. Create a list of 15 skills or characteristics that you have that are also important for success as a leader.

3. Take a personal inventory to identify the types of things that people depend on you for and/or are repeatedly requesting of you.

4. Consider the legacy that you want your life to leave behind. With this in mind, write a vision and mission statement for your current leadership role.

5. Complete the Chapter 1 activity in the Launch Points Journal to help you define where you can best focus your energy and efforts.

Employing these strategies will give you clarity on where you can make your greatest impact in leadership and how you can best use your influence.

CHAPTER 2

Learn From Everything

"Leadership and learning are indispensable to each other." – John F. Kennedy

A 2016 Gallup report entitled *How Millennials Want to Work and Live,* reveals that 59% of Millennials say opportunities to learn and grow are extremely important to them when applying for a job. In comparison, only 44% of Generation X and 41% of Baby Boomers prioritize these same opportunities (Adkins & Rigoni, 2016).

This generational distinction highlights a fundamental truth: modern leaders must embrace continuous learning, not just as a personal practice but as a critical element of workplace culture. The days of static leadership, where a title signifies the culmination of knowledge, are over. Today, leaders must cultivate curiosity, adaptability, and the humility to learn from everything and everyone around them. Typically, when someone discusses professional development, it is in reference to an in-house training, conference, seminar, or even a workplace mentor. But learning can—and should—occur in other forms as well.

Many years ago, when I was hired for my first official leadership position, I was responsible for overseeing multiple school locations. In this role, I was the newest member, not only to the team but also to the state. I had moved across the country and just finished teaching Kindergarten when I embarked on a leadership journey that became one of the most fulfilling experiences of my life.

While the job itself felt secure, the many changes I experienced with my team and in the organization in the short time I was there were unsecure. In that role for less than two years, I can't even begin to count how many different positions, teams, and leadership adjustments the organization went through.

Because I was so new—to leadership, the state, the organization, and everything I was responsible for—one of the most important things I did at the start was simply observe. Most people think leadership is all about action, but when you lack sufficient knowledge and experience, that action can sometimes do more harm than good. So, I observed. I paid attention to cues and studied the organization's culture. I noticed what was deemed as important, and I also observed what actions were actually being taken. During everyday interactions, I watched how people treated each other across departments, in different roles, and across organizational lines. Also, I listened to what people were saying and paid attention to what they weren't saying. I noted what was considered taboo and what was generally accepted.

To ensure I understood what was being communicated, I also asked a lot of questions—an immense number of questions—to peers, leadership, and those I was responsible for. I surveyed staff and team members to better understand what was important to them. After the first school year together, I wanted to reflect on what I had done well and identify areas that needed improvement. Since I had no real frame of reference, I wanted to ensure that, even if my supervisors thought I was doing a great job, my staff also felt my leadership was valuable to their experiences. I wanted to make sure I was doing everything I could to help my team succeed.

In one instance, I conducted an anonymous survey with the goal of assessing my leadership, identifying gaps, and improving processes. I asked respondents to share their positions so I could understand their perspectives as they answered the questions. That survey taught me a lot about what I was doing well and what needed improvement. But I was sincerely surprised to learn how much my team appreciated being listened to. They valued the fact that I took the time to get to know them before trying to impose any changes.

Additionally, I studied all of the requirements of my position because this organization had many layers of compliance and legal obligations. Therefore, I wanted to make sure I understood every regulation, policy, and procedure in order to do the best job possible. As my knowledge increased, my understanding of who I was working with deepened, giving me greater appreciation for the organizational culture. I became laser-focused on how important it was to pay attention more than I demanded attention.

In addition, I learned to listen more. Through listening, I turned inward to better understand myself and ensure I dedicated an appropriate amount of time to reflection. I paid close attention to my staff and everything else I needed to focus on. I viewed myself and others through the lens of the needs of the program: its requirements, recommendations, and expectations.

As a result of these practices, I committed to making learning a continual part of my effectiveness as a leader. I realized very quickly that not only did I have a lot to learn for this particular position, but I also had a lot to learn about the power of leadership, its importance, and how those things can change depending on who I am working with, the time of year, or the demands we were facing. I recognized the need to consistently consider myself as a student-teacher who is always growing, not the kind of leader who never evolves.

Throughout the survey process, I made sure to take inventory of who I was to better understand the legacy I wanted to leave behind as a leader. I learned to build and lean on my emotional intelligence because, let me tell you, leadership is not for the faint of heart. Leadership is not for people who are highly emotional or sensitive.

In fact, I had to make sure that I could navigate frustrations and rejections without taking them personally, handle the competing demands of middle management responsibility, and not feel like any of the causes of the frustrations were intentional.

Having a clear understanding of who you are and how you affect others is critical. In the same vein, it's important to decide how you want to show up and continually work on making a positive impact once you decide that you want to be effective. Once you understand how that might unfold and what it might look like, recognize that maintaining effectiveness and relevance as a leader requires continuous effort.

That's why being a student—an ongoing, perpetual student—is so important. For me, I simply had to determine what my team needed, and that's exactly what the survey helped me do. It allowed me to ask my team what they needed in a way that felt like there were no strings attached—a way that let them simply tell me what they wanted me to know. The process was completely anonymous. I surveyed everyone at the same time, then when I was alone I analyzed the data to determine how I could be as effective as possible.

Pay Attention More than You Demand Attention

Leadership isn't about commanding the spotlight; it's about lighting the path for others to achieve common goals. To do this effectively, you must learn to pay attention to the details that others miss and truly listen to what's being said (and not being said). As counterintuitive as it may seem, listening more than you speak is a worthwhile practice. Instead of dominating conversations as the authority or showcasing your knowledge, you should ask questions that allow you to glean from varied perspectives, uncover how team members think, and give them opportunities to reveal their strengths. While you are listening, pay attention to non-verbal cues to observe team dynamics, discover individual nuances, and study the dynamics of your organization and industry from the perspective of your current position. As you are gathering data, you should also begin to notice how different people respond to challenges, opportunities, and change.

An often-unintended benefit of listening is that you are also demonstrating respect and gaining insights that will help you lead more effectively. Being distraction-free and fully present in conversations and meetings creates opportunities for you to show your team members that you value their input, thereby building trust. In leadership, learning about others starts with a willingness to observe intentionally and reflect deeply.

Master Emotional Intelligence and Look Within

Leadership is more than strategy and execution; it's about how you connect with people. Popularized by Daniel Goleman, emotional intelligence (EQ) is the foundation of effective relationships. The pillars of EQ are self-awareness, self-management, social awareness, and relationship management. A leader that lacks EQ has an unstable foundation. In chapter one, we discussed the importance of deciding who you want to be as a leader. In conjunction with knowing who you want to be, you also need to have an accurate assessment of who you are currently. Self-awareness is an understanding of your strengths, weaknesses, and emotional triggers. It is also having an accurate interpretation of how your mood and actions affect others.

A great leader strikes a balance between introspection and outward observation. When managed without bias, this balance allows you to have a better perspective in decision-making and meeting the needs of team members. While observation focuses your efforts on others, introspection provides opportunities to concentrate on who you are and how you are showing up in the face of others' self-awareness. You can do this by taking the time necessary to evaluate your own strengths, investigate your areas of needed improvement, fine-tune your leadership style, and understand your priorities against the backdrop of your responsibilities. Equally as important is knowing what triggers and habits you may have that can negatively impact your interactions and decisions.

Once you have assessed who you are, you need to be able to demonstrate self-management by regulating your actions and emotions particularly in high-pressure situations. As a leader, you must be able to stay composed and intentional. Your team relies on you to lead with a sense of stability without emotional outbursts or retaliation. These negative behaviors can quickly erode trust. As it relates to social awareness, you need to be able to display empathy by considering other perspectives, recognizing group dynamics, and adjusting your approach when appropriate. The final element of EQ is relationship management, where you focus on building trust through consistency, reliability, and authenticity.

An emotionally intelligent leader is able to pull all of the pieces together to resolve (or manage) conflicts constructively and foster collaboration amongst others. Overall, leaders who excel in EQ create environments where people feel valued, understood, and motivated to contribute. EQ is so important that it should be included in every aspect of your leadership; it is also embedded throughout this book.

Ask Your Team What They Need

One of the simplest yet often overlooked leadership strategies is asking your team to define what they need. Doing this not only opens the door to meaningful dialogue, but it also positions you as a leader that listens and cares. When you inquire about your team's needs, please be prepared to act on their feedback in one way or another.

Being responsive to feedback does not automatically mean that you do exactly as asked. It only requires that you communicate your intention to take what was communicated into consideration and come up with a solution that is in the best interest of everyone. Knowing what is on the hearts and minds of those you lead will provide the needed perspective on how to approach various decisions and directives. When you are responsive to feedback, you foster a safe space for open communication. Doing so also helps you to make any needed adjustments to your leadership approach and appropriately address barriers to success.

Learn from Others and Evolve

The best leaders are also great learners. They observe others, adapt quickly, and remain committed to growth. To establish yourself as a trusted authority, embrace a mindset of perpetual evolution. Team members expect consistency in character more than they want consistency in action. With every new opportunity, you should commit to surrounding yourself with leaders who inspire and challenge you to grow. To lead well, you will need to remain open to change while

> To establish yourself as a trusted authority, embrace a mindset of perpetual evolution.

also sharing what you've learned with others. Teaching others what you are learning reinforces your credibility as a leader who is always evolving. When team members become aware that you are adapting to new technologies and maintaining an understanding of industry trends, it positions you as a forward-thinking, flexible, and trusted leader.

In a world that is always moving, a leader who has "arrived" and stops growing eventually gets left behind. Leadership is an ongoing journey of learning and unlearning. No matter how experienced you are, there's always more to discover. So, make sure that you maintain curiosity, pursue feedback, and invest in your development. When you model a commitment to continual learning, you inspire your team to do the same. To remain relevant and impactful, you must commit to learning from everything: your successes, your failures, society, your team, and even your competitors. Effective leadership and learning are, indeed, indispensable to each other. When you embrace learning as a lifelong journey, you not only grow as a leader, but you also create a ripple effect of growth within your organization. Keep evolving, keep questioning, and keep showing up as the kind of leader that inspires others to do the same.

As you continue to launch, avoid making assumptions by asking clarifying questions. Meet with team members at various levels to gain perspectives beyond your own. This will ensure that you're giving directions, issuing directives, and making decisions with an understanding of the current dynamics and workload of your team members. As you're implementing these strategies, make sure that you're meeting with your supervisor. I recommend having regular one-on-one meetings with your supervisor. It is in those meetings that you can get your needs met, state your concerns, and allow opportunities for your leader to help you develop as well.

Regardless of the metrics or tools that are in place, every leader has some unspoken expectations and definitions related to success. When you meet with your leader, ask, "Based on our needs as an organization and your needs as my leader, what does success look like in my position?" This ensures that you are meeting both the written description of your role and considering any other unwritten expectations that might either be holding you back or could serve as the catalyst to push you forward. It's difficult to meet a metric that you don't know exists, so don't be afraid to ask the questions you need to get as much clarity as possible.

CHAPTER 2 LAUNCH POINTS

1. Identify any places where you may be operating from assumptions and need clarity.

2. Determine how you might get additional input about your position (or performance) from others.

3. Outline the areas where you need to increase your skills and how you will go about doing so.

4. Develop a process where your team members can share their needs with you.

Visit www.launchtoimpact.org to access the Leadership Skill Builder Blueprint to work through the chapter two Launch Point exercises.

CHAPTER 3

Adjust Your Approach

"Leadership is a function of flexibility." — The Center for Leadership Studies

Research has identified as many as twenty different leadership styles (Cornell, 2024). From transformational to servant leadership, each style reflects different ways to inspire, guide, and influence others. But leadership styles are only part of the equation. Personality types also play a significant role in how you connect with others and provide a motivating environment for your team. Some people thrive on structure, while others crave creative freedom. Some need encouragement, while others value clear directives. As a leader, you need to understand how you show up for your team and what drives your team members.

Along with leadership styles and personality types, you can also add the various coaching approaches—directive, developmental, and collaborative—that are tailored to specific situations and individual needs. When considering all of this, you will quickly realize that one approach does not fit all. The most effective leaders are flexible, not rigid. They understand the art of adjusting their approaches based on the people they lead, the challenges they face, the conditions they work under, and the outcomes they seek.

For five years, I was blessed to work at the largest county office of education in the United States. During that time, I held two positions that encompassed multiple responsibilities. There were times when my work required me to act as a liaison, making sure that information was clearly communicated between the county office and the programs the organization contracted with and vice versa. At other times, I operated as a consultant, working with programs to identify the steps necessary to ensure the implementation of effective systems and continuous quality improvement. There were also times when I served as a compliance officer, determining whether things met the required standards or fell short. As a team leader, I was responsible for guiding internal teams to ensure the effectiveness of either a specific content area or an entire program.

Regardless of the position I held, the multiplicity of functions required me to demonstrate great flexibility. I adapted my approach depending on who I was working with and the responsibilities at hand. For example, one program administrator I worked with was very straightforward in her approach. She wanted the facts delivered directly—no sugarcoating, no good news first—just a clear presentation of the situation so we could figure out the best way forward.

Another leader that I worked with had a more supportive, coach-like demeanor, which was also the way that she received information the best. Yes, she wanted to hear exactly what was happening and appreciated openness and frankness, but the resolution phase of the work was more from a coaching perspective.

Other leaders needed me to step in as a consultant, identifying the work that needed to be done and the necessary steps so they could determine how best to steer their teams. While I was also responsible for guiding my own teams—each composed of experts in their respective areas—my role was to rally those strong, diverse personalities together to help the organization move forward. That was no easy task, to say the least. However, the one thing that almost always ensured success was flexibility. You see, not every person, organization, or team can be managed in the same way. Each individual, team, and organization requires a level of specificity and individualization to truly achieve success.

As a leader, you must pick up on the distinct but sometimes subtle cues that will help you identify the real needs of those you serve. After all, leadership isn't just about influence; a significant part of leadership is about serving the people for whom you are responsible. And so, one approach does not fit all.

One team member had been with the program for a long time and was well respected because of her work, role, and level of expertise; she had a specific niche in the organization. When I came in and was assigned to provide technical supervision, it was important that I did not try to "overlord" her; instead, I maintained and communicated a level of respect for her work.

Another colleague, a more seasoned person, came in at the same time as me. Working with her was a different challenge in that not only did she want to be respected, but she also wanted to be revered in such a way that her input was not seen as collegial but as hierarchical. In short, she wanted us to do what she said, while simultaneously not seeing us as contributing members of the team who were able to give input even when she didn't feel like we should. Working with both of these personalities required a level of flexibility and understanding that was critical to the success of the team and ultimately the organization.

One Approach Does Not Fit All

The one-size-fits-all mindset is one of the fastest ways to lose trust, credibility, and results. Your ability to pivot between approaches will directly influence your effectiveness as a leader. The first thing you need to do is consider your current context. What works during a crisis

> *The one-size-fits-all mindset is one of the fastest ways to lose trust, credibility, and results.*

probably won't work during a brainstorming session. The situation often dictates the best leadership style. For instance, a firm stance is necessary in times of crises, but collaboration is imperative when innovation is the desired outcome.

When you understand the personality styles of your team members, you can adapt to their needs. It helps when you are aware of which team members are detail-oriented versus big-picture thinkers. Another consideration is who tends to prefer working alone versus who thrives in collaboration. Knowing these things allows you to tailor your interactions and expectations accordingly.

As you grow in your understanding of your team members, you are better prepared to adjust your tone, pace, and methods. A leader who can shift between empathy and firmness or structure and flexibility is a leader who maintains effectiveness in all circumstances. When you let go of rigid approaches and embrace flexibility, you create an environment where people and outcomes thrive. If you are challenged with making these adjustments, you likely need to do a bit of self-examination because maintaining your position might be rooted in a fear of losing control or in a need to conceal insecurity.

> *Leadership requires both strength and vulnerability.*

Guard Your Heart

Leadership requires both strength and vulnerability. Leading with compassion doesn't mean that you allow yourself to become emotionally depleted, overburdened, or taken advantage of. In fact, as you adjust your approach to meet the needs of others, it's essential to guard your own heart while also remaining empathetic. Guarding your heart ensures you can give your best to others without losing yourself in the process. When working with a variety of personalities—especially someone who is more experienced, older, or more set in their ways than you are—you cannot take their reactions or responses personally. Make sure you are operating from a space where you are crystal clear about who you are and what you bring to the table. You need to approach both the individual and the situation with wisdom, avoiding the temptation to rule with an iron fist. Instead, be clear, concise, and succinct while also demonstrating both compassion and understanding.

It is also important that you set boundaries and become clear about what you will and won't tolerate for yourself and your team. Be sure not to take everything personally. Not every challenge or conflict is a reflection of you. Sometimes, people's reactions have more to do with their own struggles than your leadership. In knowing your audience, you will be able to respond with what they need most, even when they don't always realize they need it. This is why it's so important to guard your heart; you will encounter resistance even when what you're offering is what's best for the team.

Last but certainly not least, you cannot neglect self-care. To lead others well, you must first lead yourself.

Prioritize activities and habits that keep you balanced, energized, and focused. Be sure to exercise, spend time with family, get a full night's sleep, and eat regularly. You should also make time to decompress by going out with a group of friends, traveling, and relaxing. A leader that is not able to disconnect often becomes a leader that faces burnout, places unrealistic expectations on others and is in jeopardy of losing touch with the ability to maintain a variety of perspectives.

Check Your Thoughts

More than you may realize, your mindset influences your leadership. Self-doubt, negativity, or closed thinking can undermine your ability to adjust effectively. Remember, self-awareness is the first pillar of EQ. It's not enough to know who you are; you must also address the things that are not in your best interest. This requires you to embrace a growth mindset where you believe in your ability and the abilities of your team members to learn, improve, and embrace change. A major component of a growth mindset is continuously taking opportunities to develop your skills and expand your thinking. Expanding your mindset will help you reframe challenges from obstacles to opportunities for innovation and growth. By checking your thoughts, you ensure that your leadership is rooted in confidence, clarity, and forward momentum to avoid dwelling on what's wrong to a position of finding the needed solutions for making things right.

Different Phases Call for Different Tactics

Teams, like individuals, go through phases. Bruce Tuckman's model of group development—forming, storming, norming, performing, and adjourning—illustrates how team dynamics evolve over time; with each stage requiring a different leadership approach. In the forming phase, the team is just coming together, so everyone is figuring each other out. A forming team needs their leader to provide structure, clear expectations, and direction. When navigating the storming phase, the team begins to experience conflict or growing pains. At this point, the leader should be focused on addressing conflict, building trust, and fostering open communication.

As team roles become more established in the norming phase, the leader can shift to a more collaborative style and encourage team empowerment. Once the team begins performing and functioning at a high level, the leader can step back and operate as a trusted guide that no longer needs to be involved in every fine detail. The adjourning phase typically happens at the end of a project or team life cycle. At this point, it is critical that the leader acknowledges contributions and celebrates accomplishments. Understanding these phases will help you adjust your approach to meet your team where they are and guide them to success because each phase requires different tactics.

Depending on where you are as a leader—or where the organization is in its calendar year, funding cycle, fiscal term, or whatever governs the work it does—different work cycles or phases will emerge for your team. Because of these variations, you'll need to adapt with different strategies, tactics, and approaches. As a leader, you should always maintain your standards as you strive to modify your approach. You also need to adjust your expectations while keeping outcomes in mind and using an informed approach to identify team desires, meet their needs, and move forward with the mission.

Adjust Expectations Without Losing Sight of Outcomes

Leadership requires a balancing act between responding to your team's needs and achieving organizational goals. Traditionally, many leaders have focused primarily on the work that needs to be accomplished without giving attention to the people that accomplish the work. As younger employees enter the workforce, a people-first approach is critical. One of the most effective ways to bridge this gap is to adjust expectations while staying committed to organizational outcomes. In order to accomplish this, familiarize yourself with your team members' goals, challenges, and aspirations. From there, you can help them see themselves in the organization's mission and align themselves with the current objectives. As you move forward, you will also need to exercise both flexibility and firmness. Adjust timelines or methods, if necessary, but don't compromise on the ultimate goals. When you approach leadership this way, you create a sense of partnership and shared purpose.

In my work with a long-standing nonprofit organization, I was assigned a team with members who had all been working together for quite some time. The organization was in the midst of changes, and the expectations of the team had begun to evolve in ways that not everyone was ready for; and my team that was once in the performing phase was suddenly thrust back into the forming phase. In working with this team and really getting to know who they were in terms of their strengths, nuances, personal challenges, and the work areas where they struggled, I was able to modify my approach to pull everyone together. But the expectations of their positions did not change.

Each of these leaders was in a supervisory role and needed someone to help guide and bring out the best in them. Hillary, who I told you about in chapter one, was a really well-rounded individual. She needed to be pushed out of her comfort zone to recognize what she brought to the team. Then, there was Michelle, the most senior team member, who needed quite a bit of validation. She also needed her viewpoints challenged because she had grown increasingly complacent and difficult to work with. From a number of perspectives, she was probably the hardest team member to manage simply because she was closed off and sometimes operated in a manner that was unintentionally detrimental to both herself and the team.

Finally, there was Walter, who was highly logical—almost robotic—in his approach. If there was a procedure or requirement, he followed it to the letter. Walter, however, lacked the ability to flexibly apply the information he received. When working with Walter, I had to choose my words carefully to make sure he understood that new practices would replace old policies. Walter needed someone to listen, as he felt the need to run everything by me (in great detail). He also needed a guide because he struggled to connect the pieces as they related to compliance, best practices, and regulations. Although Walter had a lot of information, he didn't always know what to do with it.

To get this team moving in the right direction, I used different approaches with each person. As you already know, Hillary moved on to other pastures. Michelle eventually opened up and became a great ally. She also began to show her softer side to others, grew more flexible, and started challenging old ideas and ways of thinking that she had once endorsed. Walter had to learn some new skills to be effective, which really turned things around for him. But over time, Walter was unable to keep up due to a rigidity in his thinking and application of policies and procedures.

Eventually, Kelly joined the team, and she came with a lot of knowledge and experience that was better aligned with the new direction of the organization. The team immediately felt threatened by Kelly's abilities. My role was to show everyone how they were all an integral part of the whole and demonstrate to them how they complement each other. As the leader, I had to be intentional about addressing them as individuals while also keeping them focused on the collective mission and holding them accountable for the results of their work. Once they developed their rhythm, they became unstoppable.

Being a leader can sometimes be a lot like being a performer: you need to tap into different parts of yourself and play the role necessary to be the most effective. Some days, you'll need to be a coach, offering encouragement and support every step of the way. Other days, you'll need to be a director, providing structure and clarity. Sometimes, you'll need to be a storyteller, inspiring your

> *Being a leader can sometimes be a lot like being a performer: you need to tap into different parts of yourself and play the role necessary to be the most effective.*

team with a vision of what's possible. There will also be times when you need to lean into a more serious, dogmatic approach, particularly during moments of crises, correction, or accountability. The most successful leaders don't cling to one role or approach; they adjust, adapt, and evolve. The more you adjust your approach and ensure that what you are offering is exactly what your team needs, the more successful you're going to be. As you grow in leadership, you'll realize how incredibly important it is to modify how you show up in rooms, in your emails, and in online meetings. All of these are necessary components for your success, and they are areas where you must apply varied approaches.

Take some time to reflect on each of your team members or colleagues. Ask yourself how your approach varies from person to person, then determine if the strategy you're using is the most effective for each individual. Identify what will work best and how you can modify your approach to ensure optimal results. Make sure you're asking questions. Don't just assume you know how or why someone is answering, responding, or navigating something in a certain way. Pose questions to understand—or at least hear—their perspectives.

Last, but certainly not least, discover your primary approach and identify when you need to use other tactics. If your primary approach when leading is dogmatic, requiring certain things of people at specific times and in particular ways, understand that you may be guilty of stifling your team members. You'll need to open up a little and take your hands off so that they can begin to problem-solve for themselves. This will allow them to put things into place without being overly dependent on you. Similarly, if you are collaborative or coaching in your approach, there are going to be times when you need to tighten up so that other people can bring ideas and information to the table.

Remember, flexibility isn't a sign of weakness; it's a hallmark of strong, impactful leadership. When you learn to adjust your approach, you'll find yourself leading with greater confidence, connection, and success.

CHAPTER 3 LAUNCH POINTS

The DiSC Assessment is a powerful tool to understand personal strengths, personality types, and communication styles for yourself and your team members. The DiSC Assessment is an invaluable resource that will help you increase your awareness and ability to lead, create culture, and provide support within your organization.

1. Visit www.launchtoimpact.org to get an overview of DiSC and identify both strengths and opportunities for personal and professional growth for you and those in your organization. This activity will help you to reflect on each of your team members or colleagues. Take time to identify how your approach varies from person to person, then determine if the strategy you're using is the most effective for each individual. You'll also be able to discover your primary approach and identify when you need to use other tactics.

2. If you'd like hands-on support with DiSC, email connect@drkeena.com with the subject "LAUNCH." I'll provide you with a link to schedule time on my calendar to discuss more about DiSC and how I can support you and your team.

CHAPTER 4

Understand The Power Of Culture

"Culture eats strategy for breakfast." - Peter Drucker

Culture is more than a buzzword; it's the invisible engine driving your organization's performance. As reported by Gallup, a strong culture has the power to transform an organization, reduce turnover, improve attendance, foster safe work environments, enhance quality, and boost countless other key metrics. Ultimately, culture is the sum total of how we engage and do things (Gallup, Inc., 2025).

Research consistently shows that employees and teams who align most closely with their company culture outperform their peers who are less aligned (Watkinson & Kar, 2023). As a developing leader, your ability to understand, influence, and shape culture is one of your most powerful tools. In this chapter, you'll learn how culture works, ways to lead with your organizational culture in mind, and how to change the culture when necessary.

Organizational Culture Starts with Personal and Interpersonal Dynamics

Organizations are made up of people who bring their unique psychological, generational, and cultural dynamics into the workplace. As a leader, you tend to become a generalist in how these areas work together, so with this understanding in tow, you begin to effectively navigate the various dynamics. Unlike any other time in modern American history, there are currently at least four different generations in the average workplace. Often due to world events and the experiences in their most formative years, each of these generations (Boomers, Generation X, Millennials, Generation Z, and Generation Alpha) have varying values, communication styles, and expectations. Today's leaders must learn to bridge generational gaps and leverage the strengths of each group.

> *Today's leaders must learn to bridge generational gaps and leverage the strengths of each group.*

Individual temperaments and learning styles impact how team members share and receive information from a cognitive and social-emotional context. When you consider the diverse blend of team members in your organization, cultural sensitivity is non-negotiable. Instead of treating everyone the same, celebrate differences and ensure that inclusivity is woven into the fabric of your organization. Having regard for these dynamics allows you to foster a culture where everyone feels seen, valued, and empowered. Tailoring your approach to individual styles fosters trust and engagement.

History Cannot Be Ignored

Just like every human on the planet, every organization has a story—a history made up of values, traditions, successes, and failures. Being aware of this history is critical to navigating the organization's culture. When you understand that organizational habits and norms are often rooted in past events, decisions, or leaders, you develop a deeper regard for how a past that you were not a part of can shape present-day events.

To begin, acknowledge the contributions of those who came before you as a demonstration of respect because doing so will help you earn trust and credibility. It is a way of passively acknowledging that you value the work that occurred before your appointment and displays a level of sensitivity regarding how you will move forward with your team. To lead effectively, you must understand why things are the way they are before deciding what to change. Before this is misunderstood, I want to be clear that respecting history doesn't mean being bound by it. Effective leaders find ways to honor the past while forging a path toward a better future. They take the time to understand cultural imprints but are unafraid to challenge outdated practices when necessary.

One of my clients, Samantha, is the executive director of a Head Start program, overseeing multiple departments composed of individual leaders and teams. In her first few years with the program, Samantha was deeply focused on understanding and observing her team, but she didn't apply the same level of intentionality to how she used the information she gathered. Even though she'd identified many necessary changes in the culture of the organization and several missteps from the past, she minimized the impact these issues had on employees and how they would thwart the team's forward movement.

When Samantha gave directions, she often became frustrated because people didn't fully follow through on her requests or directives. This was simply because (based on their experience with previous leaders) they were waiting for more clarity or guidance from her. Patterns cannot be broken overnight when employees are often in situations where they're not permitted to make decisions on their own or constantly have to reach out to someone to ask, "Can I do this? What should I do? How can I...?" Previous administrators spoon-fed the leadership team, and as a result, several people were as wobbly as baby calves when it came to executing and exercising autonomy.

Because of the nature of her job, the size of the requirements, and the scope of work, Samantha wanted to have team members who could receive a quick email or text message and execute flawlessly. However, that wasn't the group she was fortunate enough to work with. Instead, she had to be fully understanding of the culture that she was facing and start from where her team members were versus where she wanted them to be. Understanding the power of culture means that Samantha's approach with her team had to lift them out of the past by modeling and supporting them to where they needed to be. Once she was able to do that, she could make much more progress with her staff.

So, although you may feel like you are unable to affect change the way you would like, you must understand that there's a group of people looking at you, waiting to see your next move. They are wanting to see how your leadership will move them forward and ensure their success. The actions that you take will help to erode, improve, or maintain the culture of your team or organization. You get to decide what that looks like. For Samantha, significant growth has occurred in the spaces where she has been consistent in her approach, communication, and understanding.

Language and Actions Shape Culture

Entering a space with a rigid, traditional structure was very challenging for me when I first started on my leadership journey. The structure in this organization was so rigid that staff felt like they didn't have permission to do anything; they were almost operating from the perspective of being robots. Employees that were tasked with distributing flyers were even required to get management approval to have the secretary make copies for them! It was like nothing I had ever seen before. As a result, I needed to go in and understand the culture. I needed to observe interactions, monitor situations, and attend many meetings to understand how the culture was impacting what was (and was not) happening in the organization and why those activities were being carried out in the way that they were.

At first, I honestly didn't understand the organizational culture quite as well as I thought I did or even needed to. There were a lot of mistakes that were made along the way. As I began to grow and understand the people and culture, I realized that I would need to take small steps with the staff in order for them to make any changes because they were so sheltered and locked into the previous way of doing things.

To begin, I started to build collaboration by understanding who the staff members were as individuals and what they wanted to see in their specific areas. From there, I was able to bring them along by getting them to learn more about the requirements and the new direction that the organization was going in. This led to a lot of repetition in building relationships and closing gaps to make sure everybody understood the next steps. In doing so, I was ultimately able to start changing processes.

One of the processes I had to change was the way new materials were ordered after old materials were discarded. I repeatedly used the phrase: "no broken anything." If you know anything about educators, they don't want to throw anything away. When I visited classrooms, there were puzzles and games with missing pieces. As I made my rounds from classroom to classroom, I literally told each teacher that there should be "no broken anything." I said this time and time again to the sound of a broken record. Then, at some point, the teachers began saying it themselves. Eventually, the directors were saying this phrase too, and the mindset around placing orders changed.

The teachers began to view their classrooms in a new way. Instead of functioning from a place of lack, those within the organization began operating with forward thinking and in forward motion. Who would've thought three simple words would've changed an organization's culture so drastically? You see, the ultimate goal was about improving quality and distributing autonomy, but I needed to start small and this single phrase was used to ignite the fire.

When you're talking about culture, there are two things you need to know. First, your actions and language shape culture. Second, repetition is absolutely necessary. So, I continued to say "no broken anything" until I didn't need to say it anymore, which opened the door for me to empower the staff and adjust their roles in ways they hadn't quite seen themselves operating in before. But modifying those roles meant I had to bring the staff up from where they were as opposed to starting them out where I wanted them to be. I didn't change my expectations, but I altered my approach. After that, I saw progress.

Next, I stopped being the answer to everyone's questions. In order to empower people, you have to ensure they understand that they have answers as well. For my team this empowerment looked like me receiving their phone calls and questions, then asking them, "What suggestions do you have?" I wanted them to see that they had the answers within themselves. Remember, they were used to doing whatever they were told and performed their duties robotically. There was a significant amount of training and development provided. But in order to make sure that staff were actually using the information they received, I had to take my hands off of some things and take more of a coaching approach. This shift to the staff owning their decision-making helped to change the organization's culture by empowering people from a place of long-standing knowledge and understanding about their roles, moving the organization to the next level. With each level of leadership, they were encouraged to empower their teams and thus the cultural shift permeated through all levels of the organization.

Language and actions shape culture. Culture isn't built on mission statements, documents that you pass out, or posters that you put up somewhere. Culture is truly created by the words and

> *Culture is truly created by the words and actions of leaders and team members.*

actions of leaders and team members. When you are looking to build, understand, and navigate your organization's culture, recognize that the language you use matters . . . but your actions matter even more. You are going to repeat the mission statement, vision statement, values, and anything else that you want others to take hold of. This is a fundamental tenet of learning.

Even more important than repetition are your actions. So many times children are led and even raised by the mantra of "do as I say, not as I do." But that doesn't work in leadership; it's ineffective. You need to model what you expect of your team members so that they see what you want them to do, carrying out expectations as their leader. Conduct yourself in a manner that aligns with your value statements—model the person that you are asking those you lead to be. Once they see you behaving in that manner, then the message you are trying to communicate will stick.

From there, you will be able to inform and shape the organization's culture. Make sure that you are also speaking in ways that reflect the culture you want to create. If you say you want a collaborative team that works together and values every team member, you need to use "we" statements instead of "I" statements. Your actions should demonstrate that you truly are a team player. Don't just go into your office and make decisions in isolation; instead, attend meetings to get ideas and input. Use all of the language that conveys "we are in this together" and make sure that people can see evidence of their input in some form.

As a leader that is trying to cultivate a culture of teamwork, you almost become invisible when reinforcing your values through consistent messaging. Again, if inclusion is a core value, then you should talk about it on a regular basis. Make sure that inclusion is evident in your actions by bringing people to the table, sharing reflections, and getting others' input. When I mention inclusion, I am not explicitly referring to embracing people solely based on race, disability, gender, or socioeconomic context. Inclusion here means to provide an opportunity for all team members to be included in some form, bringing them all to the table as integral participants in the work that is being carried out.

Do all the things that communicate that your workplace is an inclusive environment, including celebrating behaviors that align with your desired culture, because recognition helps to reinforce norms. It's often said that what is rewarded will be repeated. So, when you see those that are functioning in a way that is in alignment with the direction you want your team to go in, celebrate them.

It is important to understand that celebrating team members is not something you should take lightly. Celebrating team members is also not something you should do ad nauseum because you don't want people to go numb to the acknowledgement. To avoid this, make sure that you're celebrating people in ways that are meaningful to them. I always say, "Today's exception becomes tomorrow's expectation." When commemorating milestones along the way, don't overdo it and cause your celebrations to be minimized or drowned out.

You will also need to address behaviors that undermine the culture as quickly as possible. When you're addressing unacceptable behavior, do so in a constructive manner. You don't need to demean or diminish people for their missteps. Instead, call out the things that are not healthy or beneficial for the direction that you're leading in. Failing to address problematic actions sends the message that they are acceptable, so you want to tackle them as quickly as possible. When negative behaviors or missteps are left unattended or ignored, people begin to think that those things are permissible and this will chip away at all that you are trying to accomplish. As a leader, your language and actions are your most powerful tools for shaping culture.

Changing culture often means acting counterintuitively. When an organization's culture isn't producing results, change is essential. However, changing a culture is rarely easy, often requiring work that has never been done before. For example, if the current culture is overly hierarchical, you may need to prioritize empowerment and transparency. If the culture is resistant to innovation, you may need to encourage experimentation and celebrate failure as part of the learning process. If a culture is overly critical, you may need to focus on positivity and

Changing culture often means acting counterintuitively.

recognition. The overall idea is that you want to move the organization and team away from the unhealthy or ineffective demonstration of the past culture.

Whenever you are attempting to shift an organization's culture, you will have to be more consistent than you've ever been before because you will likely encounter more resistance and/or uncertainty. The current culture is holding the organization back, so you must determine what changes might be necessary and how you will implement them without alienating your team. Sit down with your team members and ask for their input because the more you involve them in creating the direction, the more buy-in you will have.

Communicate the "why" behind the changes as clearly and consistently as possible, making sure you recognize that changing culture takes time. Most research says it takes three to five years to change a culture, but with the right approach, you can guide your organization toward a healthier, more effective, and productive future. But doing this is going to take consistency and clear communication on your part. You must keep everyone apprised of what is happening, communicating and restating the "why." Anytime a change occurs, you're going to need to have full disclosure and be as transparent as possible so that people do not feel like you are being disingenuous or have any tricks up your sleeve. I often say once people understand "the why" then how becomes much easier.

Your team needs to know that the road to progress is never a straight line; there are going to be times when

The road to progress is never a straight line; it seems like you are going in one direction but things aren't coming together. But just because there's a hiccup or misstep somewhere along the way doesn't mean that you are failing. It means that you are going to make mistakes along the way. It means that you are human. As long as you don't have a culture that is consistently punitive when errors happen, people will feel safe and even productive.

When mistakes are made, culture cannot be delegated. As a leader, you are commander in chief as it relates to establishing, shaping, and maintaining culture. This responsibility cannot be assigned to someone else. It begins with you—your words, your decisions, and your behaviors. Set the tone for how your team will operate even if you are a new leader.

Make sure that you're leading by example. If you want a culture of accountability, you have to model accountability. *If you want a culture of accountability, you have to model accountability.* This means that you have to be held accountable as well. If you want innovation, you have to show a willingness to take risks, being open to ideas, suggestions, and ways of thinking that might be contrary to your own. Consistency is the key. People will look to you as a cultural anchor. Your inconsistent behavior will undermine their trust and make it harder for the culture to take root. It'll make it more difficult for your team to trust or follow you, so engage them directly while HR and other departments implement cultural initiatives.

Your presence and involvement will give those initiatives the weight and credibility needed to truly be successful. You have to be all hands on deck as it relates to culture because it's far too important to assign it to someone else, and in fact, you really can't delegate it to anyone else. Any cultural change requires your direct investment and influence, so you must make space for it and have the necessary conversations to keep moving in a direction that is beneficial for your team, the organization, and the goals and objectives you have set forth. Within the context of a larger organization, identify what you want your team to be known for and how you can do that in support of the larger culture and vision.

Whether your goal is to master the status quo or make a significant cultural change as a leader, you must always keep your eye and hand on _____ the culture. Culture is not static; _Culture is not static_ it evolves with every interaction, decision, and initiative. Although incredibly powerful when nurtured intentionally, culture can also be fragile. Leaders who understand the power of culture can inspire loyalty, drive performance, and create lasting impact. Remember, culture isn't just about how things are done; it's about the values and behaviors behind what is being done. Culture defines your organization.

Chapter 4 Launch Points

Visit www.launchtoimpact.org to download a bonus resource that will help you define and align your team culture.

This activity is designed to help you reflect on your organization's current culture, analyze your team's culture, and create an actionable plan to better align the two. Through this process, you will gain clarity on what your team should stand for and how to support the organization's broader vision.

1. Write a description of your organization's current culture.

2. Next, write a description of the team or department's culture, then compare and contrast the two within the context of your larger organization.

3. Complete the Culture Assessment and identify what you want your team to be known for and how it will support the larger culture and vision. Determine the elements of culture you need to focus on and what specific things you will need to do to address them. Pinpoint where you need to better align your language and actions to get your desired results.

CHAPTER 5

Navigate The Middle

"An employee's motivation is a direct result of the sum of interactions with his or her manager." - Bob Nelson

Whether you are a middle manager or supervisor, you probably know how challenging it can be to "manage in the middle." Caught between the vision and directives of senior leadership and the day-to-day realities of frontline employees, middle managers often juggle conflicting priorities, expectations, and demands.

Despite the challenges, middle management is also an exciting space. It's there that you gain the autonomy to innovate while guiding your teams through complex times (Maurer, 2023). Middle management is the bridge between strategy and execution, so when you navigate it *Middle management is the bridge between strategy and execution.* effectively, you create value at every level of an organization. I often refer to middle managers as the glue of an organization. In this chapter, we'll explore how to lead yourself, your team, and your boss, equipping you with strategies to thrive in this critical leadership role.

The Capital Gains Foundation is a well-established nonprofit organization that has made a significant impact in the community they serve. They also had a long-standing, hands-on CEO with a strong personality and multiple layers of leadership. The organization's executive team members wanted to be decision-makers, but the CEO saw that as his role. So, there was a constant tug of war between the untraditional executive team and the traditional CEO. As a result, the members of senior leadership continuously clashed.

The CEO was proud of the fact that he single-handedly hired everyone that was a part of the organization; he was the final authority on all decisions that were made. But the executive team saw this as slowing down their progress and diminishing their authority because, after all, they had worked in their specific areas of expertise for decades. They had a hard time accepting that the CEO needed to be as hands-on as they were.

In my work with the organization, although I was unable to make any changes with the CEO, I helped the executive team see themselves as the people responsible for the organization's effectiveness. Though they were not the ultimate decision-makers, the executive team became effective in making sure all objectives and initiatives were carried forward. They needed to understand that they were responsible for communicating and overseeing the vision of the organization. The executive team also had to recognize that they were responsible for creating the synergy between the multiple departments as well as the other teams that were functioning within each department. The executive team also became more effective in collaborating to ensure that they were operating at optimal levels.

Through our work together, the executive team was able to understand that their leader expected them to be responsible for all of these things while also making sure they were keeping their leader abreast of all of the challenges, successes, trends, and innovations related to their specific area of focus. Ultimately, the executive team didn't get to be the final decision-makers like they wanted, but they received a clearer understanding of their individual and collective roles as a result of our time together. They were able to communicate with their CEO in ways that they had not been able to before, and they gained a better perspective of what was expected of them in leading their teams. In the end, the goal of the executive team members wanting to be ultimate decision-makers was unrealistic. The real prize, the real victory, was understanding how to navigate their position in the midst of being the people that were reporting to a deeply involved CEO but also leading their respective departments. In time, they were able to navigate the middle.

Leading from the Inside Out

To lead others effectively, you must first lead yourself. As discussed in chapters one and two, self-leadership is the foundation for all other leadership. It requires clarity, discipline, and resilience. Once you have given attention to who you are and how you show up as a leader, you should focus on your team and your leader. Like a flight attendant who enforces adherence to safety regulations but doesn't fly the plane, your role is to implement directives, align your team, and maintain operational excellence. A good middle manager learns how to play their position by understanding the scope of their influence and focusing on excelling where they can make the most impact. Instead of wasting time and energy in spaces that are not yours to worry about, start where you can make a difference and learn how to be flexible in your approach.

Leading from the middle requires balancing flexibility with consistency. As you align your actions with your boss's directives, you need to be rigid about your values, your priorities, and the non-negotiables that uphold your organization's mission. Flexibility is available in how you achieve those outcomes, adapting to challenges and opportunities as they arrive.

> *Leading from the middle requires balancing flexibility with consistency.*

Early in my career, I adopted a personal mantra that I will offer to you: "How do I make this work for me?" As I was given information about a new initiative or project that needed to be addressed in addition to the work that I was already responsible for, I immediately asked myself that question. Once I moved into leadership, I added a layer and asked a follow-up question: "How do I make this work for my team?" This question helped me to feel less like something was being placed on me and gave me a greater sense of ownership in how I would carry out the assignment. As a middle manager or supervisor, there is sometimes little flexibility in what needs to be done, but there is often room for how you accomplish your work. How you move forward is a function of your style, values and priorities.

Leading Your Team

Your team looks to you for direction, advocacy, and consistency. As a middle manager, you're uniquely positioned to be their strongest advocate while holding them accountable to organizational standards. So, as you are leading your team, make sure that you are aligned with your boss. Your team's success depends on your ability to align their work with your boss's expectations. So, understanding your boss's priorities and goals is necessary so that you can communicate them clearly to your team; this will ensure that everyone is rowing the boat in the same direction. When you have conversations with your boss, restate what is being communicated to you in your own words because you want to check timelines and priorities to make sure you understand how all of the pieces are connected. This way, you can share that information with your team and delegate effectively.

Make sure your team understands that, in everything they do, you support them; you always have their backs. Advocate for their needs, recognize their achievements, and address their concerns accordingly. When your staff feels supported, they will perform better and stay engaged. The minute you start to move away from your role as their advocate, you will begin to encounter challenges with your team. So, you should make sure that each member of your team understands that you are their number one supporter and will do what is necessary to ensure that they are set up for success because they are a reflection of you. The actions and performance of your team members reflect your leadership.

> *The actions and performance of your team members reflect your leadership.*

If you expect accountability, you have to demonstrate it by holding yourself and your team members accountable to do the things you say you're going to do. This accountability doesn't have to come across as disrespect; it's as simple as a reminder, redirection, or conversation. If you value collaboration, make sure you're modeling that as well. Your influence sets the tone for how your team will operate, so put forward what you expect from others.

Hold individual and group meetings regularly with your team. Scheduling routine check-ins is vital for maintaining open lines of communication to stay abreast of everyone's progress and meet the needs of subgroups (if you are responsible for those as well) and each individual employee. Group meetings help to keep everyone aligned, and one-on-one meetings provide opportunities to address individual needs and concerns. Both are necessary to lead effectively.

Inspect What You Expect

Trust your team but verify that their objectives are being met. Inspecting doesn't mean that you don't trust; it just means that you want to make sure things are moving forward in the expected manner. So, establish some clear metrics, follow up on progress, and provide constructive feedback. Accountability ensures that no one feels overlooked or underappreciated so that things are not missed along the way. As a middle manager, you want to be made aware of things falling through the cracks or not moving forward appropriately when you are communicating with your boss.

At the end of this chapter, there is the Leading with Resilience and Integrity resource for you that contains questions every middle manager should ask themselves and sometimes their team. These are things, again, that you can find out through your individual and group meetings. If you're not inspecting what you expect, you will not be able to see whether the goals and objectives are being met. You won't see if your team understands how their work is contributing to the larger vision and mission, and you can't assess whether your team members are getting the support they need. You also won't be aware of any barriers that are holding you back.

In his book, *Leading from the Middle,* Scott Mautz says that middle managers are the epicenter of encouragement, meaning that their attitude and energy are contagious. Stay optimistic and solution-focused so that you can inspire your team and foster a culture of motivation and engagement. Your team members, even in the most trying times, look to you for direction, so ensure that the direction you're providing is clear and offers the hope they need to keep moving forward. In times of stress or crises, team members need to be able to approach you to receive a jolt of inspiration and energy to know that their work is not in vain—they are valued members of the team and are doing things that are important to the organization's vision and mission. Ultimately, even when they don't express it, every team member wants to be seen and valued.

> *Ultimately, even when they don't express it, every team member wants to be seen and valued.*

Leading Your Boss

Often overlooked, managing up is a vital skill for middle managers. When you manage up, you become an expert on navigating your boss, growing your skills to understand what your leader needs, building a strong relationship with your boss, and managing their expectations to maintain a delicate balance between both submission and advocacy. Successfully doing this requires communicating with your boss in such a way that they understand how to best work with you, which can be challenging but rewarding.

Pay careful attention to your organization's time-lines. Every organization has its own timelines, periods of highs and lows, and times of intensity or high input. But there are also moments when things can be a little bit quieter or in the middle of a downshift. Learn the ebbs and flows of your organization. Understand your boss's priorities and how they may shift based on what's happening with the organization, the time of year, or even what might be going on with your boss personally.

Stay attuned to the seasons of your organization and adjust your approach accordingly. Some organizations are pretty calm in the summer, but for other organizations summer is peak planning time. The holiday season is often calm for some organizations; however, if you work in retail, the end of the year is chaotic. Wherever you are, remain sensitive to the calendar and the peaks and valleys of your organization. Know how to navigate during all of those seasons and understand what your team needs to focus on to make sure that your boss's priorities are being met.

Balance the space between submission and advocacy because being a great middle manager does not mean that you are a yes-person. You need to advocate for your team when necessary, but make sure you do it in a way that is respectful and tactful. You can offer perspective on things that your manager or boss may ask for without being insubordinate; however, learning how to strike this balance is critical. When done well, you build trust and credibility with your boss. Ultimately, if your team is unsucessful, your boss is unsuccessful as well. As a middle manager, you should always be waving the white flag and making sure that you are able to point to the potential pitfalls and lead everyone involved to success.

Ask questions instead of making demands. When you need resources or support, frame your request as questions. Instead of saying, "We need more staff," which is the cry of most people, you can ask, "What's the best way to address our staffing challenges?" This approach invites collaboration and shows respect for your boss's perspective without you coming across as being demanding or dogmatic. Always make sure that you are collaborative, supportive, and active in bringing solutions when working with your boss.

> *Always make sure that you are collaborative, supportive, and active in bringing solutions when working with your boss.*

When navigating your boss and managing up, determine what things are most important to you in the season you are in and how you or your team can help to achieve those objectives. What are your top priorities? How can you communicate challenges or opportunities in a way that builds trust and partnership? When you are able to express difficulties to your boss, the element of surprise is removed. No leader likes surprises, so you want to make sure you understand how to communicate information to your boss in a way that is most meaningful for them.

Middle management is not an easy role, but it is one of the most impactful things that, I believe, any leader can thrive in. By conducting yourself with clarity, guiding your team with purpose, and leading your boss with great tact and skill, you become the glue that holds your organization together. A better understanding of your role can transform how you operate within your organization; when middle managers align with their bosses, advocate for their teams, and communicate effectively, they improve collaboration and create a more cohesive unit.

As a middle manager, you may not set the organizational strategy or execute it on the front lines, but you play a vital role in ensuring that the vision becomes reality. By navigating the middle with skill and intention, you position yourself as a leader who not only drives results but also inspires those around you.

Chapter Five Launch Points

1. Visit www.launchtoimpact.org to access Leading with Resilience and Integrity. This free resource contains strategies and reflective questions to think through including:

    - Does my team maintain regular meetings with a recurring agenda format?

- When is the best time to hold individual and group meetings?

- Are the meetings scheduled in my calendar? Have the dates been shared with all relevant attendees?

- Am I modeling the values and behaviors that I expect from others?

- How can I remain resilient and resourceful in the face of challenges?

- Does my team understand the organization's objectives and how their work contributes to those goals?

- Am I providing the support and accountability my team needs to succeed?

- What are my boss's priorities, and how can I achieve them?

- How can I communicate challenges or opportunities in a way that builds trust and partnership?

2. Make sure that you establish a regular meeting time with your leader. Using the Leading with Resilience and Integrity resource, identify at least three questions you can ask your leader at your next meeting to set you and your team up for lasting success.

CHAPTER 6

Cultivate Relationships

"Personal relationships are the fertile soil from which all advancement, all success, all achievement in real life grows." – Ben Stein

When employees have high levels of engagement, the impact on organizational performance is significant, measurable, and transformational. Research consistently shows that the quality of the relationship employees feel that they have with their immediate leader or manager is the primary driver of engagement. A study published in *PLOS ONE* found that engaging leadership positively influences work engagement and team effectiveness (Mazzetti & Schaufeli, 2022). The research highlighted that leaders who actively engage with their team members foster an environment that enhances individual and collective performance. In leadership, cultivating strong relationships is not just a soft skill; it's absolutely essential for fostering trust, loyalty, and motivation in your team. Relationships are the foundation of leadership, so the way you build, manage, and sustain them will define your success.

Early in my career, I had a leader that regularly hosted parties at her home. Although she invited several employees to the events, not everyone received an invitation. Most of the invitees on the guest list were team leaders. I was invited to the party, but I was not a leader at the time. I felt odd about going to such parties and could never fully enjoy them because I believed leaders needed to maintain clear boundaries between themselves and their employees. For me, attending those parties created a gray area.

I went to the parties feeling a sense of obligation because my boss asked me to be there. She invited me to her home. I knew the guest list was short in comparison to the number of employees that worked for the organization, and as a peer, I saw that such an absence of boundaries could impact how my boss received others. I also saw the potential conflict in situations where she needed to assert her authority. For instance, those who were invited to the party were often surprised or offended when she had to fulfill the duties of her role and position by conducting observations, reprimands, etc. They questioned the validity of her authority when they had also been enjoying drinks and having fun together with her.

This gray area is a place where I don't ever want to see any other leader in—one that I have prided myself in making sure that I have never put myself in. I saw the impact of the parties and their short invitation lists on those that were not invited. Ultimately, it was not a secret, and those that were not invited felt like my boss was playing favorites. Because certain people weren't invited, they treated the colleagues that were invited (as my grandmother would say) with a long-handled spoon. Team members who were not invited made sure to not rub those who attended the parties the wrong way, tiptoeing around and treating partygoers well so as to not get on the boss's bad side.

All of these characteristics are detrimental to cultivating genuinely effective relationships across your team and organization. It's also harmful when building trust as a leader. To foster stronger trust and connection, leaders can implement key strategies that encourage transparency, consistency, and meaningful engagement with their teams.

Build trust and respect in relationships. The most productive relationships are built on a foundation of mutual trust and respect. Without these elements, relationships deteriorate into being simply transactional, robbing teams of the connection and collaboration necessary for success. You can build trust by being consistent, leading with empathy, setting clear expectations, being reliable, and acknowledging contributions. This means, you show

> *The most productive relationships are built on a foundation of mutual trust and respect.*

up when you say you're going to show up and follow through on your promises. Communicate openly and honestly, doing what you say you are going to do so that your team will see that you are a person of your word. When you can't follow through, communicate that as well. People are much more forgiving if you are open and own your mistakes or missteps. The point isn't to be perfect, it is to be consistent and to follow-through with the things that have been communicated.

Lead with empathy. Make sure that you take time to understand the perspective of your team members. When people feel heard and truly listened to, they are much more likely to trust you and your intentions. Set clear expectations and check in with team members. People respect leaders who provide clarity, so ensure that you're defining their actual roles and responsibilities, not only going by what is listed in a job description. Every employee has a job description, or at least every employee should have a job description. But every job and team comes with some unwritten requirements. Be clear on your true unwritten expectations of your members. Then, communicate those goals and priorities to minimize misunderstandings.

Acknowledge people's contributions. I believe that what you reward will be repeated time and time again. So, make sure that you are recognizing individuals and celebrating their efforts and achievements both publicly and privately. Acknowledging contributions and celebrating successes does not mean that everyone should be treated the same way. Treat people in the way that works best for them while acknowledging their output. Gone are the days of celebrating an entire team when only half of the members actually did the work. This behavior waters down the effectiveness of your recognition for those that are actually carrying the load. Honoring those who are doing much of the heavy lifting lets them know you value how much effort they put into their work, which reinforces respect and trust in your leadership. Genuine recognition also lets everyone know that you are paying attention and that rewards are distributed based on merit and not just attendance.

Maintain respect and avoid favoritism. When one of my longtime mentors first took on her role as director, she met with each of her leaders individually. I will never forget what she said in the meeting. She started by saying, "I'm so glad to work with you," then continued to utter all of the typical fluff that is articulated during the first meeting with employees. She then proceeded to say, "One thing I want you to know about me is that my personal life is on a need-to-know basis." I was shocked when she said this because it was unexpected. I may have even been a little bit offended at the time.

Over time, I began to respect that statement so much because I realized my longtime mentor wasn't playing favorites. By making that statement, she was ultimately saying, "At some point, we'll get to the personal things, but right now, we have a job to do." And we did get to those personal things eventually. She was at my wedding, and I participated in celebrations with her. She became a great friend to me and my husband, but she made sure that the work was prioritized and respect was maintained. .

As a new leader, the first thing I want you to do is to make sure that the boundaries are where they need to be between you and your team because respect is earned over time through actions. Respect is also maintained by treating others with dignity and fairness no matter the circumstances. It is important to strike a balance between being approachable and maintaining a healthy distinction amongst yourself and your team. Being the decision-maker, you rely on your team to get things done and to give you fresh insight and information. You are the final authority and must carry yourself as such, so there is no room for favoritism.

Avoid favoritism by maintaining clear boundaries to prevent the perception of bias because that erodes trust. Healthy boundaries allow you to maintain your focus, protect your energy, and guard your objectivity. Being pulled by team members or having to navigate the gray area can lead to displays of potential bias. Maintain healthy boundaries by being transparent, modeling professionalism, and staying objective.

Avoid blurring the lines between your personal and professional relationships. I always say it is hard to hold someone accountable on Monday morning when you partied with them on Saturday night. Understand that your primary responsibility is to your team's collective success. You can go to a birthday party, but you should leave before everybody gets too excited. You can show your face at events and give baby shower gifts, but you do not need to become like one of the family. Boundaries may feel restrictive at first, but they create the necessary structures for healthy, productive relationships.

Clearly and respectfully communicate boundaries. To avoid offense or misunderstandings, let your team know your preferred methods and times of communication. Over the years, I have encountered leaders that set no boundaries regarding communication times. I had a new leader that worked incessantly. A borderline workaholic, she emailed and texted at all hours: 10 PM, 11 PM, 12 AM, and throughout the weekend. Because she worked seven days a week, she thought her team did the same. Even though I was a salaried member of her team, that salary did not equate to ownership. In fact, a salaried or exempt status never equates to an absence of boundaries.

In the spirit of managing up, I had to set some boundaries and let this boss know that communicating on Sundays was a non-negotiable for me unless there was an absolute emergency. I also let her know that Saturday afternoons and evenings were for family, leaving only a small window on Saturday mornings for her.

During the week, I created additional boundaries. I made sure to turn off my email notifications so that when I was at home working late, which happened often, I could not send or receive messages in my inbox. Essentially, I worked offline, catching up on emails without anyone knowing and protecting myself from receiving additional messages while I was trying to get ahead. Once I finished working the last thing I would do is switch my outbox back to online. Somehow that simple act made me feel so successful and it prevented anyone from disrupting my energy. You must protect your energy as much as possible by maintaining boundaries.

Maximize the lines of the organizational chart. Leadership is not a solo endeavor. You may have heard of the phrase "it's lonely at the top." Well, I always say, "It can be lonely at the top, but it doesn't have to be." Building relationships with peers, supervisors, and other department personnel is just as important as connecting with your team. When you look at a typical organizational chart, you may see lines going in different directions, associating one group or person with another. Oftentimes, you may operate like those lines are your boundaries and restrictions, but they really should be seen as pathways or connectors. Your allies on the organizational chart can be powerful assets in achieving your individual and team goals. Use those lines to figure out who you need to collaborate with and how to reach

> *Your allies on the organizational chart can be powerful assets in achieving your individual and team goals.*

those people. Look for opportunities to work with other leaders and departments to understand how powerful collaboration can be by building mutual respect and shared purpose.

Support other people's success. Another way to navigate the lines on the organizational chart is to celebrate the wins of your peers and offer assistance when appropriate. Communicate upward. Every supervisor wants their team members to support their goals and priorities. In fact, supervisors need this. A part of managing up is making sure that you align your efforts with your supervisor's goals and priorities, which will help you build a strong relationship and reputation. When you intentionally communicate what you endeavor to do, you strengthen your relationship with your supervisor and further build trust.

Resolve conflicts quickly. Because disagreements are inevitable, how you handle them matters. Anytime you are working with other human beings, you are going to have conflict, but it is wise to approach each issue with a solution-focused mindset that positions you to strengthen relationships, not damage them. Strong relationships across the organization—the organizational chart—will enhance your ability to lead, influence, and drive results.

Don't give up on the disengaged. Every leader encounters team members who seem disengaged, unmotivated, unenthused, or just unattached to what needs to be done. While it is tempting to write these individuals off or give up on them, you don't want to do that. When you give up on them, it may unintentionally send a message to the rest of the team that you don't care enough to address problematic areas. You may be familiar with the phrase "manage up or manage out." I prefer to say "manage up or manage onward."

When you say, "I'm going to manage someone out," it immediately communicates a termination or a desire for someone to quit. But when you're really concerned about your team's engagement and the success of individual team members, managing onward is a more appropriate approach. Managing onward doesn't mean that a person has to be fired, terminated, or forced to quit. Instead, it actually leaves room for you to find a more suitable place for them within the organization.

There are times when people are good employees but somehow matched with the wrong position. There are times when an organization changes its strategic goals and priorities without modifying the organizational chart to match the new directives. As a result, there are people in positions that don't fit where you're trying to go. This doesn't mean you have to throw the baby out with the bathwater. Find an opportunity for disengaged people to serve in a different capacity where they can be more productive. Once you discover that new position for them, they become reinvigorated because everyone ultimately wants to be successful. I can't think of any human being that wakes up and says, "I'm going to be the worst employee possible." But once you help your team members find success and manage them onward, you create wins across the board.

In order to re-engage disengaged team members, seek to understand them. Sit down with them, have coffee, find out what's going on with them, and try to understand their perspectives. There could be challenges that they are facing that you may be unaware of and maybe even resources that you can provide to better support them. There may be vital information that you don't know from the seat that you are sitting in that can resolve their problems. Make sure you are gaining clarity with regard to their experiences.

Disengagement often stems from a lack of direction, so help your team members understand how their work contributes to the team's goals. Sometimes, people just don't understand why what they're doing matters. They don't think it's that important. But once you provide clarity and direction for them, it gets them moving in the right direction.

Offer support. Sometimes, staff disengage because they just feel unsupported, invisible, and valueless. So, show them that you're invested in their success by offering the resources they need. Maybe they need some coaching, mentorship, or professional development. Maybe they don't have the equipment they need. Maybe there are delays in getting their work done because their computer is outdated. The point here is to make sure to offer individual team members support before you move forward with punitive actions.

Focus on the small wins. Help disengaged team members achieve small, manageable successes so that you can rebuild to boost their confidence and sense of purpose. The more small wins people accumulate, the more they will start moving toward bigger wins. While not every employee will fully re-engage (let's be honest, some people are just kind of checked out for one reason or another), your effort will demonstrate to the entire team that you are a leader that doesn't give up easily and you value your team members.

How you manage relationships is critical to your success as a leader. Leadership is inherently relational, and the quality of your connections will determine the level of trust, engagement, and performance within your team. It's often said that people don't leave organizations; they leave leaders. So, it is your responsibility, as a leader, to establish, communicate, and maintain boundaries that foster a healthy distinction between yourself and your team.

Along with these boundaries is the delicate balance of relationships that allow you to be seen as a caring, empathetic, relatable, and reliable individual. Building relationships isn't just about getting along with others; it's about creating an environment where people feel valued, supported, and inspired to do their absolute best work. By cultivating trust, respecting boundaries, and engaging with everyone—whether allies or the disengaged—you establish yourself as a leader who brings out the best in others. Leadership is about people, and when you focus on building strong relationships, you elevate yourself and your team to create a legacy of connection, growth, impact and results.

Chapter Six Launch Points

1. I've created an activity called Strengthening Boundaries and Building Approachability to help you reflect on your current boundaries, identify areas for improvement, and create an actionable plan to strengthen them. In this activity, you will identify ways that you may need to strengthen your boundaries and convey that you are approachable. Determine where you have strong boundaries in place, where your boundaries are not as strong, and where you need to strengthen those boundaries. Decide what changes you need to make and identify who your allies are on your organizational chart.

2. Visit www.launchtoimpact.org to access this resource and bonus videos.

3. If you're ready for hands-on help, email connect@drkeena.com with "LAUNCH" in the subject line. We can schedule a call to discuss ways in which I may be able to support you or your organization.

CHAPTER 7

Handle The Hard Stuff

"The quality of our lives depends not on whether or not we have conflicts, but on how we respond to them."
– Thomas Crum

"Change is inevitable, growth is optional" is a quote attributed to John C. Maxwell that is often applied to personal and organizational transformation. But I'd like to add a twist...Conflict is inevitable and growth is optional. As you continue to develop in your leadership, you will face challenges that require not just technical expertise but also emotional intelligence, resilience, and the ability to navigate difficult situations. Whether it's delivering hard messages, addressing conflict, or making tough decisions, your ability to handle the hard stuff will define your leadership legacy.

In one of my leadership roles, I was responsible for a team of newer, less experienced leaders. One of my team members, Derek, was challenged by a recurring issue he had with a particular staff member. While working together, this person was offended that Derek checked their files, went through their work, and (quite honestly) thoroughly performed his job. Derek came to me and shared the challenges he was having with the staffer. He told me the incident wasn't isolated and listed the steps he had taken in the past. As we continued to converse, I directed Derke to move forward with a disciplinary conversation because this person was at the point where she was choosing not to follow directives.

The staff person objected and became frustrated. They felt that the issue was personal and asked to meet with me. I agreed and suggested a meeting with the staff member, Derek, and myself to discuss the disciplinary action. In the past, if an employee of this organization complained loud enough about a disciplinary action, it would just go away. But that just wasn't what I was about. I was the leader that held people responsible for the organization's goals, objectives, and performance measures, yet I was also supportive of my leadership team.

When Derek and the staff member arrived for the meeting, the three of us sat while I listened to the team member and the supervisor. After they both had a chance to speak, I asked the staffer, "What is it that you would like from this conversation?"

Of course, the staffer said, "Well, I would like for Derek to stop harassing me, to give me time."

So, I went back to the requirements and previously communicated timelines - none of which were contested by the staffer. My response to the employee was, "I understand your frustrations. However, you should know that I asked Derek why it has taken so long to write you up?"

That exchange in and of itself bought me a lot of credibility with Derek because it was the first time that he had ever really felt supported by his leader. The employee shared with other colleagues that they had to do their jobs because I was not afraid to handle the hard stuff. The previous leadership did not support supervisors, so the tables often turned. As a result, the supervisors felt that their authority was constantly being second-guessed. The supervisors were often embarrassed or overruled in front of their staff even when they were following what was previously communicated.

As a leader, you have to understand that you have a responsibility to address issues when you're uncomfortable. But conflict and challenges don't have to be barriers to success. In fact, conflict can present opportunities to demonstrate leadership, develop trust, and drive growth, which is exactly what I did in that situation. Doing so requires a thoughtful, intentional approach. Even in that interaction, I was able to maintain a relationship with the person that was on the receiving end of the disciplinary action. Because conflict and challenges are not necessarily barriers to success, they also do not have to be destroyers of relationships. You can handle the hard stuff and still maintain respect and dignity.

Delivering Hard Messages

Leaders don't have the luxury of avoiding uncomfortable truths. Whether it's delivering constructive feedback, communicating a decision that will upset others, or addressing performance, hard conversations are part of the job. When delivering hard messages, you can do so by being direct but compassionate. Avoid sugarcoating or vague language. You can be clear while showing empathy by saying, "I understand where you are as an employee. However, these are our expectations," then listing those expectations. Acknowledge the emotional impact of the message while maintaining focus on the facts.

> *Acknowledge the emotional impact of the message while maintaining focus on the facts.*

Make sure you're prepared in advance. There's nothing quite like sitting down and trying to have a hard conversation that you are not prepared for. Before you begin, know what you need to say and how you'll say it. Anticipate the reactions and think through how you're going to respond. If you need to, I recommend practicing with a trusted advisor or colleague. Go to your HR director and say, "I am having this conversation and want to make sure that I'm ready." I guarantee you, HR will always be ready to practice with you because they don't want you to say or do anything that is going to put the organization in jeopardy.

If necessary, practice until you are more comfortable. I'll be honest, this is not something that you'll easily get comfortable with, but preparation will help. Create a safe environment by choosing a private, neutral space for difficult conversations and ensure that the other person or recipient feels respected and heard. You don't have to raise your voice or say anything that is harsh or demeaning, instead you want to hear them out and you need to make sure that you have communicated clearly. When I was meeting with Derek and his team member, I already knew what I was going to say and how the conversation was going to end from my perspective, but I still took time to hear the staffer out. Delivering the hard messages does not mean you have to be void of humanity.

Focus on Solutions

Hard messages should be paired with a path forward. Whether it's offering resources, setting expectations, or outlining next steps, give the recipient a way to move ahead constructively. During our conversation, Derek, the team member, and I revised some timelines because the first ones had already been missed. We also communicated how we would move forward in making sure the new timelines would be met. Additionally, we offered support as needed because delivering hard messages is less about the message itself and more about the needed outcome.

Authority Versus Aggression

Authority is an essential aspect of leadership, but authority and aggression are not the same. True authority comes from earning respect and trust, not instilling fear or intimidation in others. Aggression is synonymous with fear, intimidation, and harshness—things I do not support. I believe that every employee should still be able to maintain their dignity, self-respect, and the respect of others even in the midst of difficult circumstances. You can exercise your authority by leading with confidence over intimidation, speaking and acting with conviction while remaining approachable. Confidence invites respect, but aggression breeds resentment. You don't want to be demeaning, talk down to people, or be condescending. You want to preserve your position of authority. Those around you know you're the supervisor because of your title, but you don't have to act like people are beneath you or chip away at their dignity.

> *Confidence invites respect, but aggression breeds resentment.*

Demonstrate Fairness

Consistency is necessary in how you treat people and make decisions. When you are consistent, you reinforce your authority and show fairness in your expectations and actions. If you have a policy or procedure, make sure you follow it. If and when exceptions are made to these policies, be sure it is done so for a clearly demonstrated, communicated, and documented reason that you have the space and authority to follow through on. If you have a zero-tolerance policy for something, then it has to be zero tolerance across the board. When you are unfair in one instance but objective in another, it looks like inconsistency or favoritism, which diminishes your authority and ultimately gives away your power.

Stay Composed Under Pressure

Authority is best displayed through calm, collected behavior, especially in high-stress situations. Losing your temper undermines your credibility and creates an unsafe environment for your team members, so staying composed is extremely important. Authority is intended to be a demonstration of influence, not control. By focusing on building relationships and modeling the behaviors you expect, you'll naturally command respect and authority without resorting to aggression.

Reducing Problems and Maximizing Decisions

Two of the most important roles of a leader are to solve problems and make decisions that move the team forward. However, many leaders fall into the trap of reacting to issues instead of proactively addressing the root causes. When you are working on problem-solving and decision-making, diagnose situations before you act. You need all the information in order to truly solve a problem, so take time to understand the origin of an issue before jumping to a solution.

Ask all the questions you need to ask, gather the data that is necessary for you to review, and listen to different perspectives so that you can prioritize the big picture. When you only look at fine details, you tend to put Band-Aids on situations. Instead, focus on decisions that align with your team or organization's long-term goals and avoid getting bogged down by minor issues. Empower your team members so that they will be comfortable with bringing solutions, not just problems. This will build their problem-solving skills and reduce your workload.

If you find yourself repeatedly solving or addressing the same types of problems, it means two things: You haven't gotten to the root of the problem, nor have you empowered team members to successfully solve problems themselves. When empowering your team, make sure you're dealing with the source of the problem by prioritizing the big picture and making an accurate diagnosis of the actual issue. Learn from each decision by reflecting on the outcomes, figuring out what worked or didn't work, and using these insights to make stronger decisions in the future. By reducing problems and improving your decision-making process, you can maximize your efforts and minimize disruptions to keep your team focused on achieving their goals.

Challenging Conversations and Conflict Management

Conflict is inevitable in any workplace. Anytime more than one human being is involved, conflict will occur at some point. Conflict is inevitable, but growth is optional. When managed well, conflict can lead to better ideas, stronger relationships, and improved outcomes. In order to make this a reality, address conflict early. There is such a thing as jumping in too soon, but you also don't want to wait for tensions to escalate unnecessarily. Address conflicts as soon as they arise to prevent further issues. Just like with any problem, make sure you're getting to the root cause.

Listen to understand. Focus on understanding all sides of the conflict, not just your own perspective. There are at least three sides to every conflict: your side, the other person's side, and the truth behind the real issue (this is usually somewhere in the middle). Active listening will help you de-escalate emotions and uncover the real issues. Stay objective so that you approach conflicts with a problem-solving mindset. Avoid taking sides or letting your emotions dictate your actions. Emotions are temporary, but facts are forever. So, remain objective to address the problem completely.

> *Emotions are temporary, but facts are forever.*

Focus on common goals. When solving problems with others, make sure to emphasize that you have shared goals and interests so the focus is on the situation and not the individual. This approach provides the opportunity to deal with the specific issue and aim to move toward a place of collaboration. Conflict, in itself, is not a failure of leadership. In fact, conflict is always going to happen. If a leader never experiences conflict, I tend to wonder if they're truly leading. Conflict is an opportunity to demonstrate your ability to navigate difficult situations with grace and professionalism, so don't be afraid to manage it. Not every conflict can be resolved. Some conflicts just need to be managed.

The Importance of Having an Intentional Approach

Handling the hard stuff isn't just about reacting in the moment; it's about having a proactive, intentional approach to solving problems, managing conflict, and making decisions. Leaders who take the time to develop their problem-solving frameworks and conflict management skills are better equipped to confidently handle challenges. Your approach should be grounded in emotional intelligence. You should have the self-awareness necessary to understand how your emotions and behaviors affect others, the self-management to stay calm and focused even in high-pressure situations, the social awareness to recognize the dynamics at play in your team so that you can adjust accordingly, and the relationship management skills necessary to build trust and rapport while addressing challenges head-on.

Now, I'd love to tell you that my colleague Derek was always successful in his role. Unfortunately, there came a time when Derek had to be managed onward, and by "onward," I mean that he was no longer with the program. Derek was a stickler for procedures and processes; he held people to everything that was in writing to the point that he was reputed for it. But Derek was involved in an incident that the organization had zero tolerance for; unfortunately, it was a situation that called for immediate termination. Other employees were aware of the incident. As much as I appreciated and supported Derek, termination was the necessary route to take. Why? Because that was a part of the organization's culture—its approach—and had already been communicated to everyone without exception. And Derek had also been a part of the communication.

To preserve Derek's dignity, he was allowed to clean out his workspace after hours so that others weren't immediately aware of what had happened. Over time, other employees realized that Derek wasn't around anymore, so as employees do, they began to reach out to him. Since this incident, Derek has thanked me for not only following through on the policy but for handling the situation in a manner that allowed him to preserve his dignity. To this day, Derek and I still maintain a relationship outside of work, and it's all because of the way I handled conflict without compromising dignity.

Conflict is an inevitable part of any work environment. Research has found that an overwhelming majority, 85% of employees at all levels, experience conflict to some degree (Shonk, 2025). As a leader, your response to challenges will set the tone for your team and influence the culture of your organization. Handling the hard stuff isn't easy, but it's what separates good leaders from great ones. It's not just about resolving issues; it's about using those moments to build trust, foster growth, and demonstrate your commitment to excellence. Remember, growth is optional, but when you embrace conflict and challenges as opportunities for growth, you will strengthen your team and yourself as a leader.

Chapter Seven Launch Points

Navigating Conflict and Problem-Solving in Leadership Activity

1. This activity is designed to help you reflect on your approach to conflict and problem-solving as a leader. You will reflect on and answer the following questions:

    - What is your conflict management style (competing, avoiding, accommodating, collaborating, compromising)?

    - How have you handled conflict in the past?

    - Are you comfortable with conflict? If so, why?

    - In conflict, how do you maintain the dignity of others while also being true to yourself?

    - If you are conflict avoidant, why is this the case?

- What steps do you need to take to address your apprehensions?
- What is your approach to solving problems?
- What problem(s) do you repeatedly address? Conduct a root cause analysis to determine what issue really needs to be solved. This will enable you to empower your staff and eliminate issues.

2. To download this Navigating Conflict and Problem-Solving in Leadership worksheet and other resources to enhance your leadership skills, visit www.launchtoimpact.org.

3. If you're ready for deep work, email connect@ drkeena.com with the subject "LAUNCH" to learn more about consulting services and workshop trainings tailored to your organization's needs.

CHAPTER 8

The Journey Is Yours To Create

"Leadership is a journey, not a destination. It is a marathon, not a sprint. It is a process, not an outcome.
– John Donahoe

In order to make optimal impact, leadership must be seen as more than a destination. Strong leaders are committed to continuous learning and development. Leadership isn't about achieving a title or position; it's about creating a legacy of influence, growth, and meaningful contributions. The journey to becoming a transformative leader begins with a mindset that prioritizes progress over perfection. When you embrace this mindset and focus on engaging yourself and your team, the results can be extraordinary.

Consider these metrics. According to Gallup (2025), teams led by engaged leaders:

- show 17% higher productivity,
- report 10% higher customer loyalty and engagement,
- experience 78% lower absenteeism, and
- contribute to their organizations seeing 23% higher profitability.

The data is clear: engaged leadership has a tangible impact on people and organizations. But this level of engagement requires you to commit to your personal journey and recognize that leadership is a process, not a destination.

The impact is yours to make. Leadership is born out of who you are and shaped by what you do. It's a continuous cycle of learning, growth, and action. At its core, leadership is about moving from success to significance. Success is focused on achieving favorable or desired outcomes, but significance is having meaningful influence and lasting effects. To move toward significance, leaders must focus on building impact. By "impact," I'm referring to influence, momentum, problem-solving, accountability, collaboration, and tenacity.

Influence

Influence is more powerful than your position. True leadership doesn't come from your title; it comes from your ability to inspire and influence others. You must know how and when to toot your own horn. You have to be okay with highlighting your contributions in an authentic, meaningful way. As a new leader or a leader that has been promoted, highlighting your contributions does not always come easy, nor does it always feel natural. But you must become comfortable highlighting your contributions in a manner that doesn't come across as boastful but instead as a reflection of your accomplishments.

Influence is earned by demonstrating competence, empathy, and consistency, which is why it's important for you to be able to talk about the gains you have made in your career. People follow those that they trust, not those who demand compliance. When you are able to demonstrate what you can talk about, what you have done in the past, and how you can replicate those things, trust will ensue.

Momentum

Momentum is created in every moment. Leadership is not about one grand act. You don't do one thing well one time and earn respect and trust for a lifetime. Leadership is about consistency, so you need to consistently show up and make progress no matter how small that progress might be. So, celebrate all of the small wins. As those small wins accumulate, momentum increases. From there, you can use each interaction, each decision, and every challenge as a stepping stone toward your goal.

Leadership is not about one grand act.

Problem-Solving

People don't just follow leaders who point out problems; they follow those who solve them. Anyone can see when something is wrong, but not everyone has the ability to right the wrong. So, be proactive in identifying and addressing challenges in your area of influence and focus on solutions that align with the needs of your team and organization. If you're solving problems that your team isn't concerned about or impacted by, then you won't be able to build your impact or momentum. It's important that you follow through on the things that matter most to your team—the things that are going to slow their progress, hold them back, or get in their way.

Accountability

Accountability is an essential two-way street for building trust and maintaining credibility as a leader. Make sure you're holding yourself accountable for your actions and decisions, and encourage your team to take ownership of their responsibilities and results. You should not show up for your team as perfect, finished, or complete. Doing so makes you appear distant, untrustworthy and disingenuous. Team members need to see the authenticity in your leadership, which means seeing you as a fallible individual just like them.

Collaboration

Collaboration is critical because leadership is not a solo journey. The best leaders know the value of collaboration and shared success, so make sure that you foster an environment where ideas are welcomed and teamwork is prioritized. Build alliances across departments and with stakeholders to achieve common goals. Collaboration is instrumental in helping you to navigate "your place in the middle" and (as discussed in chapter 5) to build alliances throughout the organizational chart.

Tenacity

Tenacity will help you endure the journey. It is the fuel that keeps leaders moving forward even in the face of obstacles. Good leaders don't fold easily, so make sure you recognize that setbacks are part of the process. Tenacity provides the stamina necessary to withstand frustrations and disappointments. Stay focused on your vision and remain persistent in your pursuit of it. Tenacity isn't about force; it's about intentionality and showing up with purpose every single day, even when the journey feels long or uncertain. Tenacity keeps you when reaching your goals isn't enough.

From Success to Significance

The shift from success to significance requires a deeper understanding of what it means to lead effectively. It's not enough to achieve goals. Leaders must strive to create meaning and make a lasting impact. When people join organizations and teams, they are signing up for a vision and a mission. As a leader, it is your job to help them achieve the organization's goals, but it is more important that you create meaning for them within the context of those objectives. The goals, relationship, meaning, and context are going to help team members reach their own level of significance as part of your team and organization.

Leadership is about who you are, not just what you do, so your authenticity, values, and ability to inspire others will determine how significant you will be as a leader. You should allow your integrity to shine by building trust through consistency, honesty, and ethical behavior. Make sure that you are focused on your level of emotional intelligence to lead effectively by cultivating self-awareness, empathy, and the ability to manage your relationships.

A leader that is unnecessarily stubborn and change-resistant is a leader that won't last very long or go very far. Be prepared to adapt to change, overcome obstacles, and maintain focus in the face of adversity. Flexibility and resilience should be part of your genetic makeup.

Sometimes, you're going to lose. As I've said before, progress is not a straight line. Leadership is a journey filled with highs and lows, so there will be moments of failure. There will be times when things don't go as planned, leading you to question your own abilities. These moments do not signify the end of your journey; they are a part of it. Failure can be a great teacher when you view every setback as an opportunity to learn, grow, and return stronger. Your job is to identify those lessons and how you can move forward.

When I started my education career, I was focused on being a great Kindergarten teacher. In a conversation with someone that was diminishing my role as a teacher, I recall saying "Maybe one day, I'll be a teacher of teachers." Looking back on those early years, I didn't even have the vocabulary to describe what would ultimately become my destiny. I was very happy as a Kindergarten teacher, but then one day, I just wasn't anymore. The job no longer fulfilled me, and I knew it was time to move on. Usually the next step for teachers is to become some type of curriculum specialist, coach, or school administrator. Some people even pursue work as a counselor. Even though I had all the necessary credentials to fill several of those positions, it never seemed like what I was supposed to do.

More than a decade later, I realized that I wanted to work as a consultant and college instructor. My path has not been the typical route, but it has been an incredible journey—one that I have created on my own terms. Up until now, I have had many opportunities that have all led me to build a powerful network, a rich body of experiences, and the skills necessary to be a positive force for my clients and students.

Everything along my journey has guided me to where I am today. And the same can be true for you. You, too, can create your journey on your own terms.

Leadership is not a one-size-fits-all path. It's a deeply personal journey that reflects your unique values, experiences, and aspirations. All of my experiences have led me to become a great college instructor and an even better consultant and leadership coach.

As you curate your journey, keep your eye on your end goal to ensure alignment. Success is about achieving outcomes, while significance is about creating a legacy. You don't have to define that legacy today. Your significance will come from the collective influence of your decisions and experiences, and this occurs over time. Leadership is a journey that requires commitment, courage, and the willingness to develop. With every promotion, you will need more commitment, more courage, and more willingness to grow. The road may be long and challenging, but the impact you create along the way will be well worth it. As Franklin Covey says, "Begin with the end in mind." So, take the first step, and remember, the journey is yours to create.

> *Success is about achieving outcomes, while significance is about creating a legacy.*

Chapter Eight Launch Points

1. For additional resources and guidance on crafting your leadership legacy, visit www.launchtoimpact.org and download the Defining Your Leadership Legacy worksheet.

2. When completing the activity, identify what you want your leadership legacy to be and where you want to end up. Remember, your response can (and probably will) change over time.

3. Email me at connect@drkeena.com to explore consulting services and workshop trainings to further support your leadership development.

CHAPTER 9

Cultivate Your Network

"Everyone should build their network before they need it." – Dave Delaney

Understanding what you bring to the table and how it shapes others is a fundamental step toward cultivating a powerful network. Valuing what others have to offer and recognizing how those things matter to your collective growth are equally important. Networking is not a transactional endeavor; it is a relational one. Strong authentic connections can serve as bridges to new opportunities, mentors for personal and professional growth, and a reservoir of knowledge and resources.

Networking is so much more than collecting business cards or connecting on LinkedIn. It is the process of developing mutually beneficial relationships that allow you and others to thrive. Building a network starts with self-awareness and grows through intentionality and reciprocity. I began to understand the power of a strong network at my first full-time leadership job. Because of this experience, as I continued in my career, it became important to me to build relationships with the right people while contributing to strong professional associations and being the beneficiary of those relationships.

I am not a person that appreciates the traditional thought of networking. Instead of going to spaces with large crowds and events to "work the room," I prefer intimate connections with people that are made over time and produced from repeated interactions—something that all involved will mutually benefit from. In my first leadership role, I worked with leaders and peers from many departments. The organization had six different divisions and once a quarter, all of the middle managers came together for professional development. During these sessions, we created a network of support for ourselves.

That time was beneficial for me because I was able to hear perspectives from people that were doing similar work as me but in different contexts. This really helped me to see the transferable nature of leadership skills and strategies; it also gave me an opportunity to build relationships with people that I didn't engage with on a daily basis. Over twenty years later, I still maintain some of those relationships.

From that experience, I learned that a robust network has benefits that extend far beyond my immediate career needs. Networking is about positioning yourself as both a contributor and a collaborator. When you focus on relationships rather than transactions, you create a network that supports you in times of need and celebrates with you in times of success.

Here are some lessons and strategies to build and sustain a meaningful network:

- Start with self-awareness. Before reaching out to others, take inventory of your strengths, skills, and experiences. Become aware of the value you bring to others and identify the knowledge, skills, or connections you can offer to your network.

- Know what you need from others by determining where you can benefit from mentorship, advice, or collaboration. A clear understanding of yourself ensures that your approach to networking is intentional and authentic.

- Build genuine relationships. The foundation of effective networking is authenticity. People are more likely to connect with and support you when you show genuine interest in them.

- Listen before you speak and pay attention to what others are sharing. Understanding their needs and goals will help you find ways to add value. When you listen to what people are truly saying, you're able to identify their needs. From there, you'll be able to pinpoint their interests and where you can add value. After that, you can connect. So, focus on quality over quantity.

- It's better to have a handful of strong, meaningful relationships than hundreds of surface-level connections. This also gives you an opportunity to foster those strong, meaningful relationships.

- Networking isn't about meeting someone once; it's about maintaining a relationship over time. Sending a quick message, sharing an article of interest, or scheduling regular check-ins are all ways you can continue to build a connection with someone that you thought you would only see once in a blue moon.

- Give more than you receive. One of the most powerful principles of networking is to give without expecting anything in return. Offer your help by sharing your expertise, pro- *Give more than you receive.* viding materials, or connecting someone with a resource or another colleague within your network.

- Be a problem-solver by looking for ways to assist others in overcoming challenges or achieving their goals.

- Celebrate others' success by acknowledging the accomplishments of those in your network. When you invest in others, they will be more likely to invest in you when the time comes.

- Expand your circle strategically. While it is important to strengthen existing relationships, you also need to seek new connections that align with your goals and interests. As you grow, your network should do the same. You can do this by attending industry events. Conferences, workshops, and seminars are all great places to meet like-minded professionals. You can also join professional organizations.

- Become a member of industry-related groups or associations that can open doors to valuable connections and give you more exposure within your chosen field. Make sure you leverage on-line platforms. Use tools like LinkedIn to connect with people in your field or area of interest, but remember to approach online networking with the same measure of authenticity as in-person interactions. Don't just use the online space for transaction-focused endeavors.

- Diversify your network. A strong network isn't limited to people in your immediate circle or industry. You can grow and become a more well-rounded leader when you find like-minded individuals outside of your industry, particularly in leadership. I always say, "If you're an educator, you need to be reading leadership books that are not related to education. If you are in business, you need to be reading leadership books that are related to some other area of leadership. When you only focus on your industry or area of expertise, you limit the knowledge that you can have."

- Seek mentors and look for individuals who can provide guidance based on their experiences to stretch you in ways that you may have never imagined before.

- Engage with peers by building relationships with people at similar stages in their careers who can also offer support and different perspectives. Just make sure these are people that want to grow professionally like you do. You never want to engage with peers that are not going to be positive influences in your career but will require you to be focused on supporting them instead.

- Connect with rising stars. Don't underestimate the value of connecting with those who are just starting out; you never know where they may end up. I can't tell you the number of times people have discounted me, yet at some point, I became the decision maker on the other side of the table. Offer respect to everyone you encounter.

- Be intentional about following through. The strength of your network depends on your ability to follow through on your commitments. If you offer to help somebody, make sure you do it. Trust is built when people know they can count on you. Trust is lost when people realize they cannot.

- Keep track of your connections. If you need to use some type of document to do that, then make sure you do that. One of the things that has saved me a million times over is putting a contact in my phone and including a note about how I met that person to jog my memory. Lately, I have even started attaching photos to contacts. Keep a record of the key details about contacts and interactions so that people don't feel like a number when you're talking with them. It's great when you actually remember the things you need to know about them and the interactions you've had.

- Be consistent. Relationships require nurture, so a one-time encounter won't build a lasting connection. Send an email, text message, or even a greeting card. Writing letters should not be a lost art because letters communicate to the receiver that you've intentionally taken extra time for them.

The power of your network is critical. I cannot imagine reaching the level of success that I have without my network. The people I've connected with over the years—worked with and helped develop—have served as the ladders for entry into each of my next steps. My grandfather used to always say, "Don't burn your bridges. You never know when you have to cross back over them." I can tell you that my previous mentors have challenged me to embrace leadership and pursue advanced degrees, yet I can still go back to these same leaders if necessary.

My first experience as a college instructor was an opportunity that I didn't even know existed. A colleague (who was not a college instructor) actually recommended that the department chair contact me based on their relationship and her respect for me. My largest consulting contracts came from people I worked with in previous roles but hadn't seen for many, many years. Because I maintained the network, displayed respect, and carried myself well, people were quick to refer and reach out to me. Former students and mentees who are now sitting in decision-making roles have become valuable sources of referrals for me. Networking looks far beyond the current moment and career advancement. My network continues to provide resources, information, and opportunities, and these relationships thrive because I gave to others before they were even in a place to give to me.

> *Cultivating a network isn't just about achieving personal success.*

Cultivating a network isn't just about achieving personal success; it's about building a community where everyone grows together. Your network will challenge, support, and open doors for you if you invest in it with authenticity and generosity. As you develop your network, remember that each connection is a step toward something greater. Every conversation, collaboration, and shared experience contributes to the legacy you are creating. So, build intentionally, nurture consistently, and always lead with value.

Chapter Nine Launch Points

1. Use the LISTEN Framework to reflect on your current networking practices. Identify areas of improvement and strategies to enhance your interactions. I've created a resource to help you with this.

2. Visit www.launchtoimpact.org to download the Networking Guide and the Building Connections Through Networking and Reflection activity.

3. Email me at connect@drkeena.com to explore consulting services and workshop trainings to further support your leadership development.

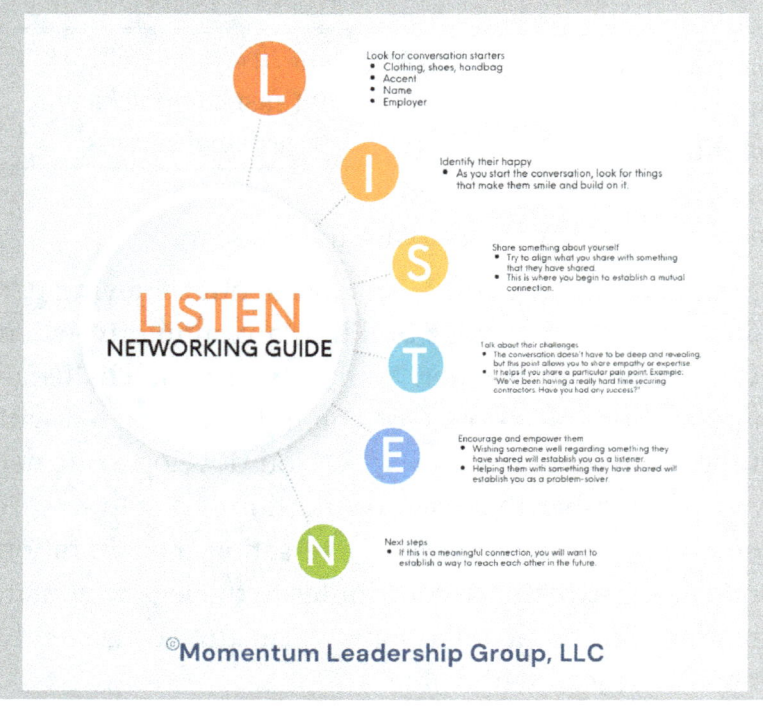

Identify the steps you're going to take to expand your network and what you will do to add value to those in your network.

CHAPTER 10

How You Start Is Not How You Finish

"To sustain longevity, you have to evolve."
– Aries Spears

In his book, *The Seasons of Life*, Jim Rohn talks about how different times in life demand different actions. He emphasized that what you do in one season will set the stage for success in the next. His ideas made me think about how a career can also experience various seasons—each with its own set of challenges and opportunities. These phases—spring, summer, fall, and winter—are integral parts of any journey, contributing to the larger picture of growth, learning, and development.

Much like the changing of the seasons, no career or leader stays the same. In fact, once you stop evolving, your career is effectively over. Successful leaders know how to adapt to the seasons, using each one as an opportunity to grow and set the stage for what is next. The key to longevity is evolution. Continually pushing yourself and refining your approach are critical so that every season positions you for the one that comes after it.

It's often said that success leaves breadcrumbs, but success also has linkages. When I look over my own career, I can see how all of the pieces and positions have come together. I started out as a part-time afternoon preschool aide at a small program that served less than 30 children, but during the summers, nobody ever wanted to step up when the director went on vacation for two months. As a result, I was assigned the interim director responsibilities each summer. She didn't just do it haphazardly or as a process of elimination; she did it because the team members trusted, supported, and believed in me. In that early season of my career, I had no idea what was going to be in store for my future.

Next, I became a kindergarten teacher. I was given various leadership opportunities in that role, and my administration encouraged me to return to school to acquire a leadership credential. I didn't go back to school at the time, but while I was a kindergarten teacher, I also had several volunteer leadership roles at church. I even led church leaders across the state.

I got my first official leadership job because of those experiences and volunteer ministry roles that I put on my resume, grabbing the attention of my then-soon-to-be supervisor. Once I secured my first supervisory job, I was responsible for school across multiple locations and cities. See the connection?

From there, every leader in every position I had saw something in me that I didn't see in myself, and with each position, those leaders encouraged me to move to the next level. Every position I have ever secured has included seasons of opportunity, challenge, expansion, high productivity, reflection, and even preparation.

Spring represents opportunity, challenge and expansion. In the early stages of your career, you are likely entering a new role with fresh opportunities. You might even be expanding your responsibilities, but this phase of growth can be both incredibly exciting and overwhelming. Like the blossoming flowers of spring, everything seems new and full of promise. However, this season also requires an open mind and a strong willingness to learn. The learning curve is going to be steep, but you must embrace it. Spring is about laying a foundation. You will be discovering your new environment, establishing relationships, and understanding the intricacies of your role. Be intentional about everything that you're learning, whether it is through formal training or simply by observing those around you. The first responsibility of a leader is learning, so pay attention and make sure that you're taking everything in.

The first responsibility of a leader is learning.

While you're doing all of this learning, work to establish your vision because the spring season is about setting goals. What do you want to achieve in your new role? This is your time to dream big and set the course for seasons to come. Even if you've had prior leadership roles, this new position requires you to establish your vision and identify the type of leader you want to become.

Summer is about stretching and development. In the summer season, you may feel a sense of stagnation, and this might be a little bit challenging for you. During this time in your career, you may feel like you've outgrown your role or maybe even your current circumstances. Quite frankly, you might even be a little bit bored or feel disconnected. But, don't fear. Summer is a time for you to stretch yourself, obtain new skills, and prepare for the next phase of your journey, so embrace the growth that summer holds. If you feel like you've outgrown your role, look for some new challenges and maybe even seek opportunities to grow in ways that you hadn't thought of before.

Summer can feel like a quiet season, but it's one of the most powerful for you personally and professionally. You can prepare for new beginnings. Summer prepares you for fall, so take some time to consider what the next chapter of your career will look like. Whether you're going to take on a new role, enhance your skill set, or reevaluate your long-term goals, summer is the season for preparation. Don't let your summer go to waste because fall comes next.

Fall is all about productivity and harvest—a time when you hit your stride. In fall, you will be deep in the thick of your work, and things will move at full speed. Your productivity will be at its peak, and you will begin to see the fruit of your previous efforts. Fall is when you make your mark, influencing those around you and showcasing your skills. With higher productivity comes a greater sense of responsibility, so you want to make sure that you're focused. Ensure that you're working smarter, not harder. Prioritize your tasks and align your efforts with your long-term goals. Be careful not to just be busy. Instead, make sure that you are intentional with every effort.

As your responsibilities increase, so should your ability to delegate.

As your responsibilities increase, so should your ability to delegate. Be careful not to be the leader that takes on all the responsibilities and becomes overwhelmed. Empower your team and trust them with important tasks. Make sure you're leading with a sense of purpose for yourself and your team. A leader who knows when to step back and let others shine also becomes invaluable.

Next comes winter, a season of reflection and refinement. As your career progresses, there will come a time when things will feel like they've reached a steady rhythm. You've established your systems, built a reliable team, and put processes in place. While this is a season of stability, it's also a critical moment for reflection.

During winter, look back at what worked and what didn't so that you can refine your strategies. It's not just important to know what worked well—you also need to know why it succeeded. It's not enough to identify what didn't work. You need to identify the pitfalls in each of those failures so that you can refine your strategies in a way that will allow you and your team to have continued success. So, take the necessary time to reflect individually and collectively. Ask yourself the tough questions about what you've achieved so far and the lessons you've learned. Make sure that you're still aligned with your original goals. Winter is also a time to determine if new goals are necessary.

Reflection is key during this period because it allows you to ensure you are on track for the next phase. Winter is a good time to streamline and optimize. This is when you can focus on efficiency and ensure that your systems and processes are as effective as possible. Winter is not about creating new things but making what you already have even better.

Are leaders born or are leaders made? This is an age-old question. Within this debate, I believe there is some truth to both sides. I would say the answer is both. Leadership is something you are born with to some degree because there are inherent qualities that some people just naturally possess, like charisma, vision, and decisiveness. But leadership is also a skill that can be developed and nurtured over time through experience, mentorship, and consistent self-improvement.

If you look at children on the playground, you often see some early signs of leadership. Kids organize games, encourage others, and make decisions. If you pay close attention, you'll notice that there tends to be the same children organizing the games, encouraging others, and making decisions. These tendencies are their innate leadership qualities that become refined over time through various experiences.

The making of a leader happens in stages. It happens in the seasons, and each stage of life and career presents opportunities for growth. How you navigate those opportunities determines the type of leader you'll become. As you move through each season of your career, I encourage you to embrace the joys of every phase. Spring is about opportunity, challenge and growth. Summer is about preparing for what's next. Fall is about productivity and making an impact. And winter is for reflection and optimization. Every season holds its own set of lessons that will help you evolve.

As you revisit your career plans, don't be afraid to make necessary changes. Never extinguish your dreams. This is a time that is rich with possibilities—so much so that you can try almost anything at least once. As I've said before, your journey is yours to create, so embrace it fully and finish in a way that makes you proud.

As I reflect on how to finish, I can't help but think about how my journey has kind of been a step-by-step process of moving forward in the same career path. I also think about several former staff members who were laid off due to a loss of grant funding. Many of these team members took this forced transition and used it to reinvent themselves. One was a phenomenal dancer who started teaching dance classes, launched a fitness line, dances for events (like the Super Bowl) and when she and her husband welcomed their second child, she opened her own child care. Another team member went full time with her HR consulting company while another started a home child care. Jillian, who had loads of personality and could talk to anyone, decided that this was an opportunity to pursue her dreams as a realtor and build her real estate empire. Another supervisor who was excellent with community partnerships realized that this was her opportunity to run far away from supervision responsibilities and as a result has leaned into career options that suit her preference to build community relationships.

All of this happens because each of these people realized that how they started did not have to be how they finished. Your leadership will evolve, and your journey will progress. Just as seasons change, your career and impact will continue to grow, shift, and transform. The key is to keep moving forward and embracing each season as it comes.

Chapter 10 Launch Points

1. Complete all the reflection activities at the end of each chapter to deepen your insights. These activities have been compiled into the Launch Point Journal to guide you further on your leadership journey.

2. Revisit this activity periodically as your goals and seasons evolve.

3. To download the Launch Point Journal, which includes the reflection activities for each chapter, visit www.launchtoimpact.org.

4. To explore consulting services and workshop trainings designed to support your leadership growth and development, email connect@drkeena.com with the subject line "LAUNCH" to discuss how I can support you and your team's leadership growth and development.

Closing

Now that you have reached the end of this book, you have learned how to lead your organization with clarity and courage, creating a culture of success for years to come. Be sure to put these strategies to work. I promise, you will see changes in both your organization and your impact.

When you implement these practices, you will lead with more confidence, increase your self-awareness like never before, and navigate the complexities of your work with increased ease and assurance. I encourage you to apply these foundations repeatedly throughout your leadership journey. These strategies are not meant to be used just once; instead, they are enduring principles that will support you every step of the way.

In this book, you have learned methods to establish a strong foundation for your leadership journey. Here's a brief breakdown:

Chapter 1: More Than a Title: In this chapter, you learned the difference between influential power and positional power, as well as how effective leaders create significance and have a lasting impact.

Chapter 2: Learn from Everything: Learn the importance of paying attention more than you demand attention and listening more than you speak.

Chapter 3: Adjust Your Approach: The one-size-fits-all mindset is one of the fastest ways to lose trust, credibility, and results. Your ability to pivot between approaches will directly influence your effectiveness as a leader.

Chapter 4: Understand the Power of Culture: Explore how culture works, learn how to lead with regard to your organization's culture, and determine how to change it when necessary.

Chapter 5: Navigate the Middle: Learn how to lead yourself, your team, and your boss, equipping yourself with strategies to thrive in this critical leadership role.

Chapter 6: Cultivate Relationships: Build trust by being consistent, leading with empathy, setting clear expectations, and acknowledging contributions.

Chapter 7: Handle the Hard Stuff: Leverage your technical expertise, emotional intelligence, resilience, and ability to navigate difficult situations.

Chapter 8: The Journey Is Yours to Create: Create a legacy of influence, growth, and meaningful contributions. The journey to becoming a transformative leader begins with a mindset that prioritizes progress over perfection.

Chapter 9: Cultivate Your Network: Building a network starts with self-awareness and grows through intentionality and reciprocity. Develop mutually beneficial relationships that allow you and others to thrive.

Chapter 10: How You Start Is Not How You Finish: Leaders who sustain success know how to adapt to different seasons, using each one as an opportunity to grow and set the stage for the next. The key to longevity is evolution. Every season should be positioning you for the one to come.

Don't let this book be the end of your journey. Implement what you've learned and let it be the beginning of a transformational path toward growth and success. Take action, stay consistent, and watch your efforts shape you into the leader you envision.

About Keena R. Mosley, EdD

An experienced leader, consultant, and speaker, Dr. Keena R. Mosley is committed to empowering others to bring their authentic selves to life through leadership. She uses a nurturing yet realistic (and sometimes no-nonsense) approach to engage individuals to maximize their potential and stretch to better versions of leadership with the ultimate outcome of engaging teams and meeting program goals.

At the core of everything that she does, Dr. Keena is a teacher. A career educator and lover of learning, she has served in early childhood education since 1991. Beyond her start as an afternoon aide, she excelled to fulfill several leadership roles including Program Coordinator, Learning Community Facilitator, County Team Leader, and Chief Operating Officer of a multi-million-dollar/ multi-funded child development program. Dr. Keena's work has spanned across school districts, private programs, colleges, county and nonprofit organizations, as well as state and federally-funded programs.

No matter her role, Dr. Keena focuses on personal growth, organizational effectiveness, problem-solving, and ways of providing support for leaders. Utilizing program data, industry trends, organizational analysis, systems theory, and an understanding of human development, Dr. Keena has positively impacted individuals and organizations across the United States.

Her life's work has led her to serve as the Chief Transformation Officer of Momentum Leadership Group, a consulting firm focused on providing leadership development and organizational improvement solutions to nonprofit organizations and early childhood programs.

Along with numerous credentials and certifications, Dr. Keena holds a bachelor's degree in early childhood education, a master's degree in organizational leadership, a doctorate in educational leadership. She is also a certified life coach.

www.MomentumLeadershipGroup.com
www.DrKeena.com

References

Adkins, Amy and Rigoni, Brandon. 2016. "Millennials Want Jobs to Be Development Opportunities." *Gallup.com*, October 29, 2024. https://www.gallup.com/workplace/236438/millennials-jobs-development-opportunities.aspx.

Cornell, Dave. 2024. "20 Types of Leadership Styles." *Helpful Professor* (blog). January 3, 2024. https://helpfulprofessor.com/types-of-leadership-styles/.

Gallup, Inc. 2025. "What Is Organizational Culture, and Why Does It Matter? - Gallup." Gallup.com. October 11, 2024. https://www.gallup.com/workplace/327371/how-to-build-better-company-culture.aspx.

Hayes, Julian, II. 2024. "CEOs Quit in Record Numbers in 2023. Here Are 3 Solutions." Forbes. February 26, 2024. https://www.forbes.com/sites/julianhayesii/2024/02/26/the-great-ceo-resignation-of-2023-3-keys-to-improving-ceo-well-being/.

Kilmann Diagnostics. n.d. Overview: Thomas-Kilmann Conflict Mode Instrument (TKI). Retrieved February 26, 2025, from https://kilmanndiagnostics.

com/overview-thomas-kilmann-conflict-mode-instrument-tki/

Maurer, Roy. 2023. "Unshackle Middle Managers to Thrive in the Future of Work." *SHRM*, December 21, 2023. https://www.shrm.org/topics-tools/news/middle-managers-thrive-future-of-work.

Mazzetti, Greta, & Schaufeli, Wilmar B. 2022. The impact of engaging leadership on employee engagement and team effectiveness: A longitudinal, multi-level study on the mediating role of personal- and team resources. PLOS ONE, 17(6), e0269433. https://doi.org/10.1371/journal.pone.0269433

Shonk, K. 2025. Conflict-management styles: Pitfalls and best practices. Program on Negotiation at Harvard Law School. https://www.pon.harvard.edu/daily/conflict-resolution/conflict-management-styles-pitfalls-and-best-practices/

Watkinson, Allan and Kar, Rohit. 2023. "Organizational Culture: What Leaders Need to Know." *Gallup.Com*, September 20, 2024. https://www.gallup.com/workplace/471968/culture-transformation-leaders-need-know.aspx.

www.ingramcontent.com/pod-product-compliance
Lightning Source LLC
Chambersburg PA
CBHW061806120626
46550CB00005B/2155